RAISING GOATS

A Step-by-Step Guide to Raising Healthy Goats for Beginners

By Jason Howard

By reading this document, the reader agrees that under no circumstances is the author responsible for any losses, direct or indirect, which are incurred as a result of the use of information contained within this document, including, but not limited to, — errors, omissions, or inaccuracies.

Table of Contents

INTRODUCTION

The breeding and selling of animals has gone on for many thousands of years. But, many modern people are unaware they can raise a farm animal at their house. Lately, however, the methods and manners governing the process have evolved. This book provides all the step-by-step information you will need to raise goats properly.

Like any other domesticated animal, a goat is a precious mammal that needs care and love from humans. They can, like many animals, share a sweet bond with their owner. However, there are also possible pitfalls. You may have a dog or a cat as a pet, but having a goat is very different. Goats can be tricky to handle. Many new breeders, companies or individuals, may face multiple issues when raising goats for the first time. If you, by any chance, are looking to buy and raise baby goats then please proceed to read this book.

The common problems, tricks and caring methods required to raise a baby goat into an adult will be given within the pages of this book. It will provide you with the knowledge and ideas to not only take care of them as individual creatures, but also about how to give them the best environment where they can thrive and grow to be healthy, fit and active. Whether you want to start up a business, set up a homestead or a farm, or if you just want an unusual pet, this book provides a detailed guide to every aspect of goat raising, caring, and handling. It also covers all the potential mistakes, common and uncommon, that new owners may make. Keep reading and all your questions, queries and confusions regarding these amazing animals will be answered.

I am sure you will find many things to surprise and delight you as we begin the journey of understanding these unusual creatures. I'm delighted to have you with me as we begin our exploration of the remarkable, intriguing - and often downright hilarious - world of goats. Good luck!

CHAPTER ONE

WHERE TO START?

Long before religions, races, and extremists divided the earth, men and women were few and healthy. They would work under the guidance of a higher power who, in return, would give them what they needed to live. This was a time when humans were given a chance to serve and be served. They asked the higher power to give them children of their own flesh and blood. The babies they pulled out of their wombs wouldn't always get on with their parents. They would cry and misbehave. They would become difficult toddlers with awkward mood swings. Humans found that their own flesh and blood would grow up to become rebellious teenagers, demanding things they never had themselves. Once grown into adults, they would find a spouse, and live on their own, leaving the old humans alone to die. The cycle was painful and soon the new humans realised how asking for more children would be an ungrateful wish. They thought of ways so that they wouldn't waste the chance to ask the higher power for something that would be of use.

When enough time had passed, the higher authority decided to help them. Humans asked that the one beyond them should give them something he alone would decide upon. This was humanity's way of asking for a different gift, since their last request didn't turn out quite as well as they'd hoped. As if he already knew, the higher power sensed what could be best for humankind. A quintessential man prefers to have an item of interest which would love, respect and benefit him. It doesn't have to necessarily be of human ancestry, since humans are prone to being treacherous and demanding. The higher power provided humans with a source to feed and benefit them. An animal that lacked the negative qualities that could be burdensome to humans. It was a goat.

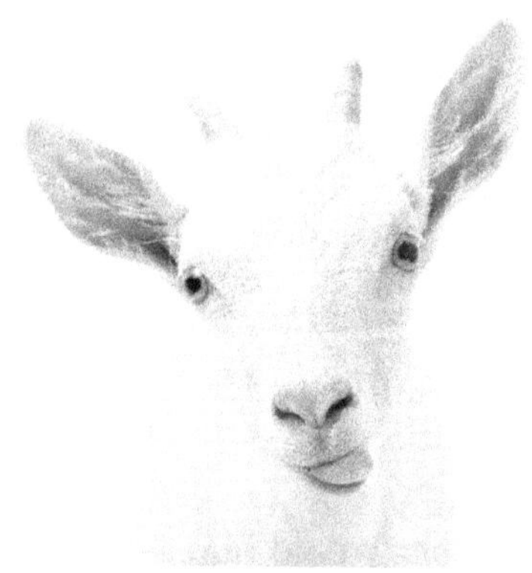

Later, when humans grew to esteem the positive qualities of goats, they asked for more. The authority handed them animals each century. However, humans later became more deeply obsessed with worldly issues, and the higher power had to let go of them. Humans developed a habit of mishandling every gift that was provided for them, except one. The first gift from the higher power - goats. These animals continued to serve mankind, and to gain his love. To date, this animal has proven to be a source of multiple benefits. An animal who so generously gives us meat and milk is little short of a miracle.

Goats have been the subject of scientific research for years. Goats are mammals, and belong to the genus Capra. They are closely related to sheep, but have some advantages over them. Male goats are called bucks or billys, and have a beard; female goats are called nannies. Goats can be pets, although they are more often regarded as farm animals. Whether you acquire them as pets or for commercial reasons, their friendly nature makes them fun, and a good companion for humans. Domestic goats mainly produce milk, and a large portion of this milk is used to make cheese.

History of Goats

It is hard to know when the first goat took its steps upon the earth. After all, it took science many years to form clear ideas about the first man. Discussing the advent of goats would likely take ten more centuries, and maybe with no definite result whatsoever. However, we believe the domestication of the first goat occurred about ten thousand years ago, in the Mesopotamian culture of the Tigris-Euphrate rivers. Researchers believe goats might well be the first herd animal to be widely domesticated, followed, some time later, by sheep. Domestic goats were usually found in mountains and forests, in Central Asia and the Middle East, particularly the areas from Turkmenistan to Turkey. The goat species is known as Capra hircus. Bezoar ibexes was one of the breeds of goats native to the Taurus mountains between ten and eleven thousand years ago in the Middle East. This was followed by the process of natural selection, in which the species became more suited to its new niche. These changes were adapted in the whole genome due to human selective mechanisms, but they still retained some of their wild properties. Neolithic farmers started keeping herds of ibex to get milk, meat, and materials for clothing. Later, goats became increasingly popular for their fiber, dairy products and meat. Today, nearly 300 breeds of goat exist in the world, and these resilient little animals can be found on all continents, including Antarctica.

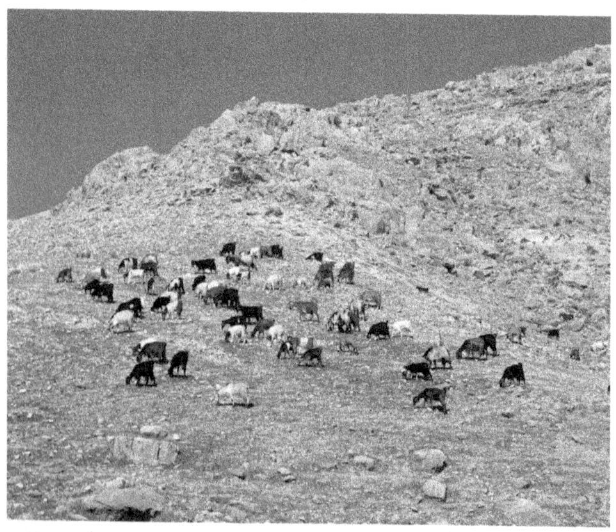

Domestic goats came into existence through evolution and natural selection. The first wild species domesticated by modern humans were from the Bovidae family. These goats, which can survive harsh climate and altitudes, were made to live in warm circumstances. This family shares many characteristic traits which makes them similar, such as herbivorous diet and type of horns. Goats, ibex, and sheep, which belong to the subfamily known as Caprinae, are considered to have diverged from other bovidae mammals as early as the late Miocene period, which reaches its greatest diversity in the Ice Ages.

Where did Goats Originate?

Were it not for Asian culture, the world might never have recognized the origin of this beautiful mammal. Had there been no evidence, such as symbols or icons with goat-like structures, we would have never realized the true origin of goats. It is also possible that the animal we currently see is much different from the original being. Selective mechanisms, provided by humans to domesticate the mammal, may have altered its behavior, physical features, or physiology. The records suggest that goats originated in Western Asia and the Eastern European mountains. Archeologically, domestication in goats has been recognized, due to the abundance and presence of the animal in areas that were beyond Western Asia, and by changes in their shape and body size that differentiate wild and domestic groups. Although, in fact, complete domestication has never really been achieved, since the animal still retains some wild characteristics even down to the current day.

Divergent Goat Lineages

The Neolithic period shows clear indications that the people of this era had domesticated goats. Traces of the animals' presence have been discovered in many archaeological sites around the Mediterranean Sea, and in Asia. This trend very likely reflects the shift whereby humanity moved from a hunter-gatherer culture to a more settled and self-sustaining way of life. Plenty of current-day studies have shown that the early mammal is different in many ways from the current species. Thanks to modern science, genetic studies have given clear insights about its lineage. When mitochondrial analysis from nineteen ancient goats was analyzed, it was found that two highly divergent types coexisted. The results agree with the scenario that in the early Neolithic periods, in Europe and the Near East, at least two independent origins, and perhaps many more remote types, existed.

There are four divergent goat lineages today, shown by mitochondrial DNA sequences. Scientists suggested there can be broad diversity in the breed bezoar ibex, or there can be four domestication events. Like any other mammal, goats have evolved. This present generation is also changing as they are not getting the feed, water, and altitude, they used to get in mountainous rural areas. Experts say that modern domestic goats are physically closely related to sheep. For thousands of years, goats were used for their hair, meat, skin, and milk. Quite cunningly, humans have exploited every aspect of this remarkable treasury.

Goat Domestication

This is the process by which domestic goats came into being by natural selection. The first species domesticated by humans were wild goats. Domestic goats are an important species for biomedical applications, and for building the economy of the nation. A superficial knowledge of goats suggests they only provide meat and milk. But, in actual fact, they are more than skin, flesh, and secreted milk. Goats can even be said to have contributed their skin, bones, and even their blood, to the world economy. At opposite extremes, their bodies can provide fertilizers, while their horns are used as delicate showpieces. Their tough physique makes them heavily relied upon in third-world countries where harsh climates make it difficult to raise and sustain other herd animals. Their relatively small stature makes them much easier to transport as well. Nowadays, developing nations rely greatly on this hardy little mammal. One estimate believes that almost 75% of these nations' economies are due to the skin trade of goats and cows.

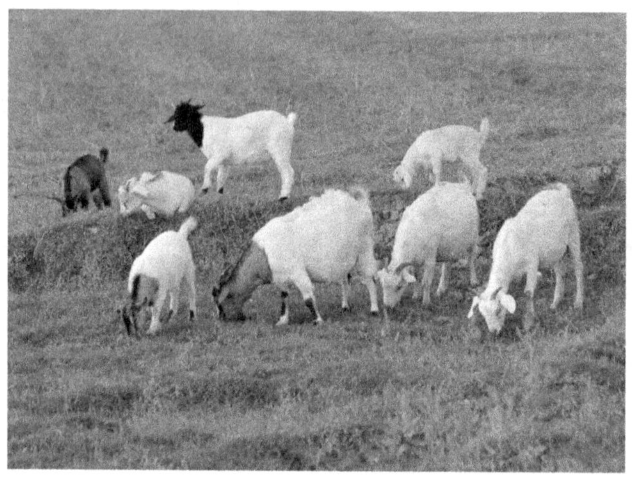

Scientific studies have proved there is a genetic diversity between Bezoar, the ancient wild goat, and the goat that lives today. The main domestication centers were near the Iranian Plateau, but due to lack of space there is little chance this could be responsible for the domestication of large numbers of goats. There must have been other facilities that helped in domestication. Another center, much nearer to Eastern Anatolia, has been discovered. This facility was much bigger and more effective than the aforementioned one. It ranged up to the northern side of Zagros, and appears to be the biggest and most likely origin of domesticated goats of this era. Therefore, the Anatolian range is a very plausible hub for the domestication of goats.

From this central area, goats gradually spread worldwide. The impulses behind this were probably a combination of trade, theft, and the movement of tribes from place to place, accompanied by their livestock.

Wherever humans went, they often took goats with them.

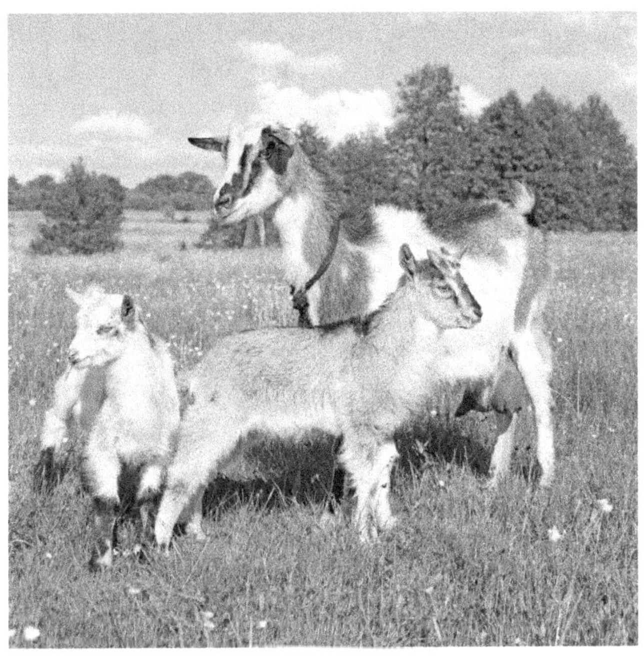

Domestication provided early men with meat, milk, skin and even fuel. Neolithic farmers would build shelters out of goat skins, and use the animals bones as weapons to defend themselves. The domestication of goats was very likely similar to other animals. Goats altered their behaviour as interaction with humans softened their wildness. Various ways were implemented for the animal to understand and accept the presence of humans. As a result, the goat would turn towards the human for help. This, no doubt, encouraged a sense of love between the two.

Domestication was done in different ways. The owner would leave the goat with a box filled with its food. However, the box would be locked, and the goat would initially become frustrated and angry. Finally, the animal would realise they were incapable of opening the box. The goats would stare at their humans, entreating them to open the case. This is similar to how dogs would look at humans, with appeal in their eyes. When the human would come forward to help, he would become a savior to the hungry goat.

Another process of domestication was a little different. Human body language would be used to check the response of the mammal. The half-tamed goats would attack the farmer when his back was turned towards them. But a human facing the animals face would seem helpful towards them. He would look attentive and obliging to the goat. In return, a goat would accommodate itself to the farmer, and opt to be helpful to him. This supports the theory of animal dependence on humans. The goats would show greater willingness to accept human assistance to solve their problems. This type of assistance is most specifically visual in nature.

The early domestication of goats resulted in broadening their physiology through selective breeding. Thus, the next generation of goats produced more milk and meat. They became denser in terms of production when compared with their wild relatives.

Where to Purchase Goats?

Are you looking to buy goats for your farm? Goats can be bought from other farmers at wholesale markets. Sometimes finding a rare goat breed according to your specific needs is difficult, but it's worth the effort. Some sources can be:

Local feed stores: Become familiar with people who work at local feed stores. They will very likely know the farmers near the locality, and are ready to send customers to them. They will also have a notice board with livestock business cards. This can be a good place where you can start your search for goats.

Agriculture papers: To look for goats that are for sale in your area these publications are a good place.

Craigslist: To find a goat locally, and with a competitive price, Craigslist is a good place. For that you have to go to the website, select a city that is close to you, and look up the farmer sale section.

Breeders' Websites: Find the website of the people who breed different types of goats by directly going to their websites. Just tap in the type of goat and the word 'breeder'. A number of websites with pictures, pedigree information, and the sale price will come up. Some breeders' websites also include additional information helpful for raising goats.

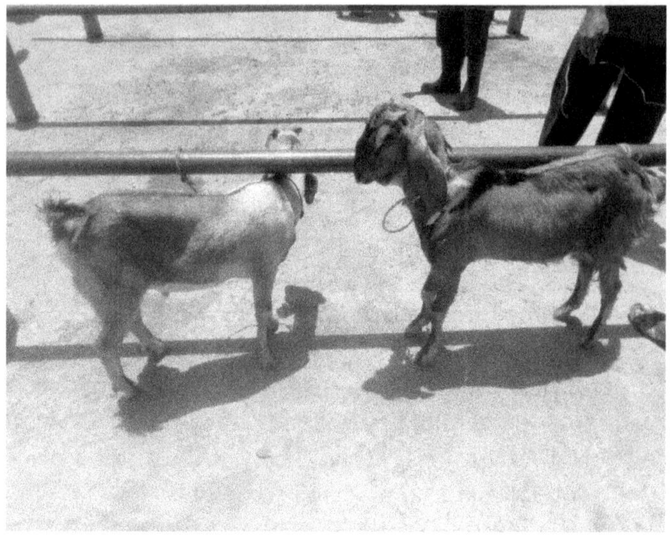

Farmers should know the current market price and the quality. They should focus on the expense and the time they are giving to their animals, and from this, calculate the correct price of their animals to maintain their business.

How Many Goats Should be Bought?

This depends on various factors. What is the reason for buying the goats? Is it because the buyer just loves goats, or they are being bought for commercial reasons? These are the factors which affect how many goats should be bought. If it is because the buyer loves goats as animals, then at least two should be bought. This is because the goat is a social animal and it is happier with a partner. If the buyer wants to start a business, even then he shouldn't buy too many goats. If the buyer has no experience of keeping goats then it's better he should initially buy a small number, and, with time, learn how to take care of them. When the buyer is confident in taking care of goats, then he should go for more. Another factor is how much space does the farmer have? As a rule, there should be at least twenty square feet per goat for sleeping indoors, and thirty square feet for exercise. A point to consider is that if someone has never looked after herd animals before, and wants to start, then goats are a good animal to begin with.

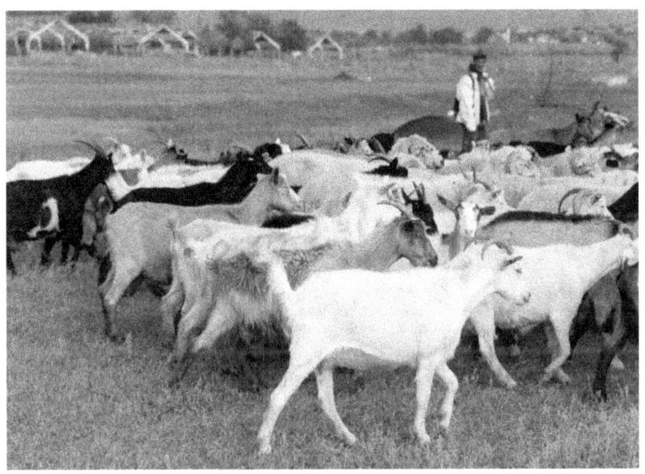

How to Choose a Goat?

Buying and raising a goat depends upon the owner's purpose. If someone wants to eat homegrown meat or drink fresh milk, they would want to choose a goat and raise it. Buying for more ambitious reasons might involve different criteria. There are some other traits that should be considered

Size: A small homestead should choose a miniature breed.

Horns: Goats with horns can hurt other goats, people and property.

Registered or not: If you want to make a farm or breed goats, you have to get your animals registered and they should have a breeding history. But, if you only want to raise them at your home to get meat and milk, you don't need to get them registered.

Breed: The type of goat matters as well. You can't breed a mountain goat, otherwise known as a markhor, in a townhouse.

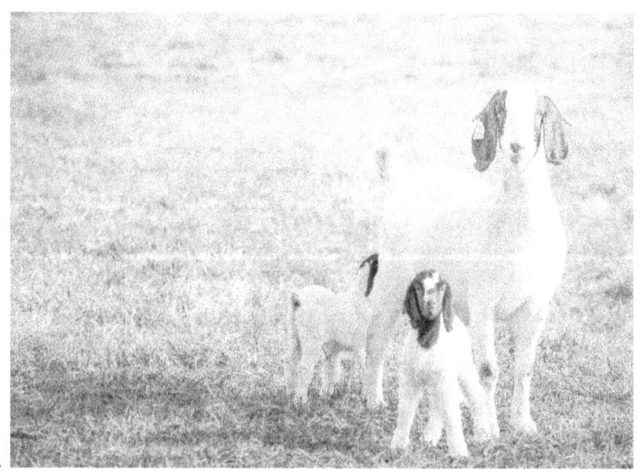

.

How to Buy a Goat?

A good quality goat is not too hard to find, but you will need to look in the right place. People make quite a lot of mistakes in purchasing a healthy goat, so you will need to make sure you don't fall into any traps. In order to find a good quality goat, your local farmers' market is one of the many places to look. You will find people selling goat cheese, goat soap, and goat milk. Those people will guide you, and give you some very good referrals.

Secondly, you can do a Google search for your neighbourhood's breeder, and if you have some particular breed in your mind, you can search for that exact type. But be sure about the breed you are going to buy. Ask locally about the breeder's reputation and their record. Good breeds are healthy and perform well. Ask yourself: How old is the goat? Why it is here for sale? Does the goat have any disease?. Examine your goat; it should be healthy and should have a solid walk. Signs of ill health in a goat can include: rough coat, big knees, and thin body. When you buy a goat, keep them separate for a month from any already existing herd. In this way you can be assured it isn't going to spread any disease, or bring parasites, to the rest of your herd.

Thirdly, you can go to local farms in search of your desired goat. You would see a lot of options there, or you can simply find someone who is experienced in this, and who will guide you to the best goat you need. A simple tip is that you will find some really excellent quality goats in small-scale farms and not on Craigslist. Why? Because Craigslist only have goats that are great for pets. That might be fine in itself. But small-scale farms have goats for all purposes; pets, milk breeds, or meat breeds.

Why a Registered Goat is Important

People don't really think goats need to be registered, but it is a good idea. For example, if you have a dairy goat for a homestead, then the amount of milk produced will be tracked. This record will help in studying the animal's parents; if the mother and grandmother gave a lot of milk, then there's a good chance your goat will give a lot too. It's true registering goats will cost some money, and at some point, you might feel you don't need all these papers, and you just want to go and visit your homestead. But, here is a thing to remember: if you are buying goats for dairy, then you will be breeding them. You will be raising their kids for several generations. Consider these starters as the main focus of your little farm, and when you buy something that holds a promise for the future, it's in your own interests not to compromise on anything. So, you would want to buy a good quality goat, as that will ensure, whether you want them as pets or as diary animals, that they'll be healthy and active. With proper shelter, food and care, they'll give you the results you want. Use some extra dimes and invest in animals that are of good standard.

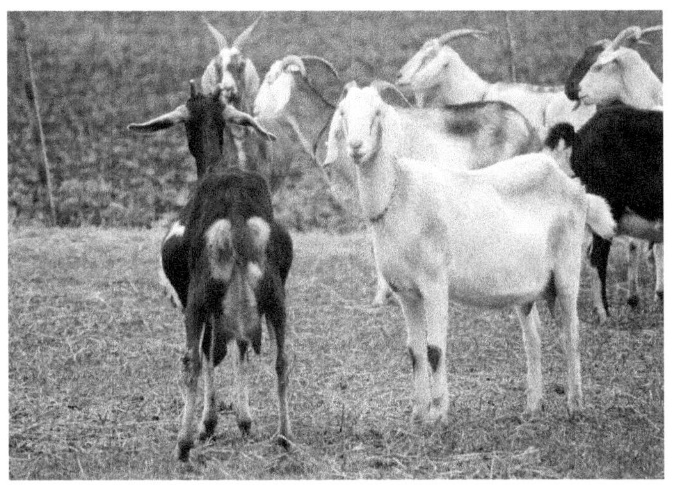

What to Look for when Purchasing a Goat?

If goat farming is a hobby, or you want to do commercial goat farming, then some tips should be considered that can save money. Commercial goat farming is very popular nowadays, and one can make solid profits. To be a successful goat owner, the following things should be kept in mind.

Business plan: Some basic learning and knowledge about goat farming, marketing management, and plans

Profit: How much profit can be gained by buying and selling of goats?

Goat breed: How to select a healthy breed.

What Things to Look for While Purchasing a Goat?

Normally, when you go to purchase a baby goat or a milking goat you need to check the facility, the fencing, the shelter, the animals around them, their feeding facility and how they get water. These things would tell you how all the animals are taken care of in that particular farm. But, as a beginner, what questions would you ask while getting yourself a baby goat or an adult one, or about the breeder themselves?

- First of all, you must ask about diseases. What diseases has the farm ever had? Check for those diseases too. Whichever specific goat you want to buy, ask whether it has any disease.

- Then you would check the goat's nose, features, and also make sure the ears don't stand up; they must be flapping downwards.

- You should check the goat's back is as straight as possible, the rear must not end in a great dip. Use your hands to check that the hips are wide because that would help out with the delivery of the baby and will help to store more milk in its udders.

- Also, check the udders are attached a little higher. The attachment must be wide so it doesn't swing or bounce too much when the goat runs.

- You also must check that both the udders are of the same size so that one is not smaller or larger in size. You can check this by standing behind the animal.

- Check the animal's ribs, they must be wide to store maximum food.

- For buying males, you must check that it has a wide stance which would be passed to the future generations. The male's mother would give the idea what its future generation would be like.

- In case of baby goats, their back must also be straight and large, and their stance wide.

- If the goats are registered they would have a tattoo on the inside of their right ear, and the left ear would show the year.

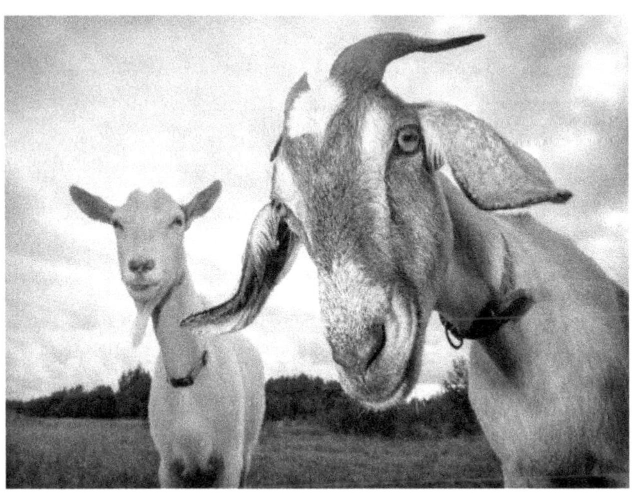

What Mistakes Should Not Be Made?

People make a lot of mistakes while purchasing their goat because they don't have any experience in it, or because they can't find someone who can guide them genuinely. Here are some tips to help you not make those mistakes.

- Never buy the first option without thoroughly checking all the animals and making sure it is actually the kind of goat you want. If you think that you would buy a goat you have seen on Craigslist, and bring it home without thoroughly doing your survey, then you may be hugely disappointed. Some goats are escape goats, or bad-milking goats, or simply sick, but if you didn't do your research, you might well end up paying the price. So, don't pick the first goat you find - take your time. .

- If you want a milking goat, do your research and never pick any goat without actually getting it on the milking stand or milking it. In fact, you can tell the farmer you will come back in the milking season. Tell the farmer you want to see the milk, the quality of the milk, and the animal when it milks. Don't hesitate to ask the farmer to show you all these things, and let you taste the milk. Also check the teeth of milking goats; two big teeth are a big thumbs-down.

- Another mistake people commonly make is to disregard the animal's annoying traits and habits. Don't ignore them when they bleat too much, or when you see a baby goat jumping for bottle-feeding; they may look cute, but the chances are this trait won't go away, and can be a serious nuisance, particularly when they grow to be a 90-pound adult goat.

- When you go to any farm, don't ignore the surrounding animals. Look for any animals who are infected or sick, and who might have passed this illness to the goat you want to buy. Do your research as to what a healthy goat looks like. You do not want to bring a sick or infected goat to your homestead.

- The last tip is - don't rush. You will want to make goat cheese or goat soap or sell your goat's milk, and develop your business to a bigger level, but you will need to start slowly. Do your research thoroughly and go shopping. Don't ignore anything odd or not normal. That way you will be able to get the best animal for your farm, or as a pet.

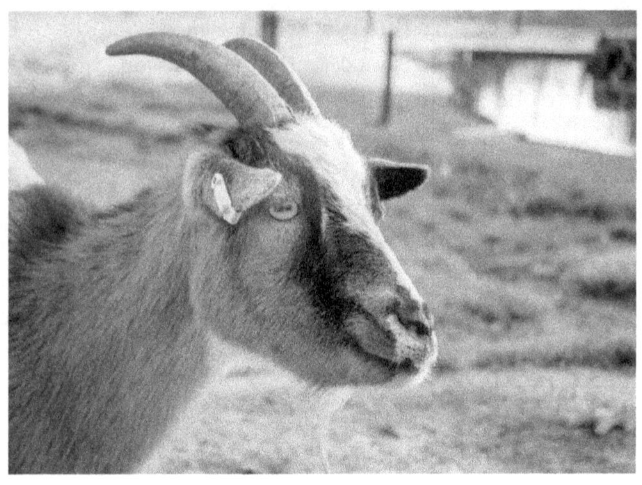

Can You Make Money Raising Goats?

There are no rocket science formulas to starting a small business using your goats, but these basic tips will benefit you. Firstly, you must decide which direction you want to go. You can either choose meat goats or dairy goats. Then you will have to set up accounts on social media websites like YouTube and Facebook. You can make a lot of profit if you want to go into dairy goats. Alphine goats are good for this purpose. The tip is to not raise your goats specifically for milk, but to use their milk to make other dairy products. There are many states where selling goat milk is illegal, so what you can do is make something else out of that milk and sell those products. Goat milk soaps are really good and in demand. But you can make any dairy product you want, and sell them from your farm. Go for products which appeal widely to people and market them properly.

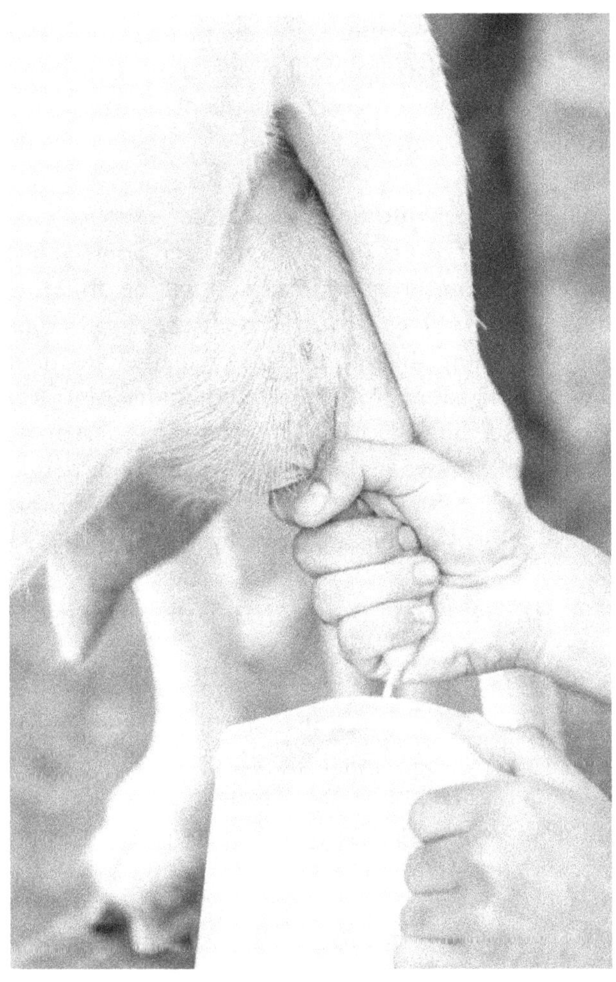

The second way you can generate profit is by selling goat meat. Goat meat ranks number one world-wide when it comes to consumption. But for this you will need to have a lot of land with quite a number of goats. And you will need to make sure they utilize their full ability to grow. But again, you can do this on a small level if you are marketing your products properly. Marketing on social media platforms will give you more profit than marketing them locally. Social media platforms give you access to a larger audience.

The number one tip to make money from raising goats on your farm is through registered goats. The tip is to invest more up front, and you will be able to sell your registered babies from that registered mother up to three times more than an unregistered goat. People are willing to pay more for a registered animal, and it will profit you so much more. You will need to learn about the genetics, and which bloodlines are more in demand. A simple online check of the registered world will amaze you at the prices people are charging.

Are Rural Goats Better than Urban Goats?

The value of a goat is dependent on its health and that, in turn, derives from its lifestyle and diet. In rural areas, mainly villages, goats are released in the morning and are taken to their fences at night. They are free to roam until evening. They spend the whole day feeding on fresh green grass and drinking fountain water. By contrast, goats in urban areas are kept locked in a small roofed farm where they can't walk freely and their diet is average. The water they are fed is not pure either. As a result, the goats raised in rural areas tend to be healthier, and their breeds are more valuable, than the goats that are raised in urban areas.

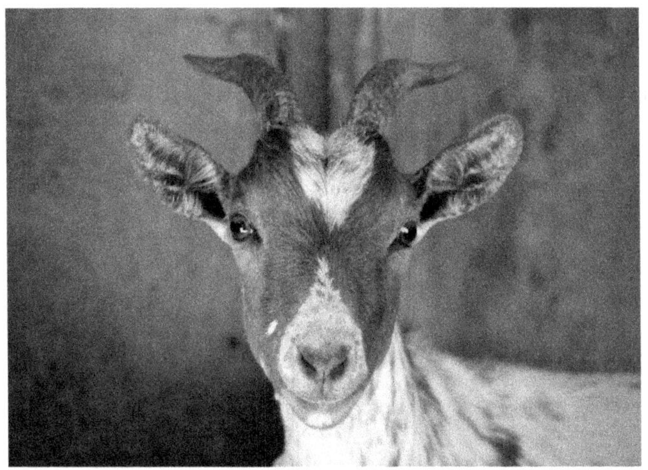

Water is the Key

Mostly goat farm owners in urban areas don't realise the importance of clean water until their animals begin to suffer from viral diseases. Water can easily become the source of many diseases if it's unclean. Water is the easiest medium that diseases use to get inside the victim's body. Essentially, common sense and expert opinion should tell you to give them the kind of water you yourself would drink without hesitation. A good tip is to have your goats' water bucket hanging slightly off the ground. Goats can be rather clumsy creatures, and do have a tendency to knock buckets over. If the buckets are hanging, this problem is avoided.

Ideal Housing

The housing for goats should be dry and have good ventilation. An ideal shelter for your goat should protect it from rain and sun. The shelters are usually over a large area, allowing the animals to roam and stay active. The floor of the shelter should be 2-3 meters above the ground. A drainage ditch should be put in the corner to help drain the rainwater during the rainy season.

Experts usually follow the practice of making the housing open without any walls or fences, this provides the goat a mental idea that it's free, and it can roam around and feed itself. The roof should slope so that rain water won't get trapped. The material which is used in the making of the roof is usually a composite made from thin cement sheets Sometimes, though, goat keepers prefer to use tin sheets for the roofing as well; they are cheap, durable, and can be changed easily whenever needed.

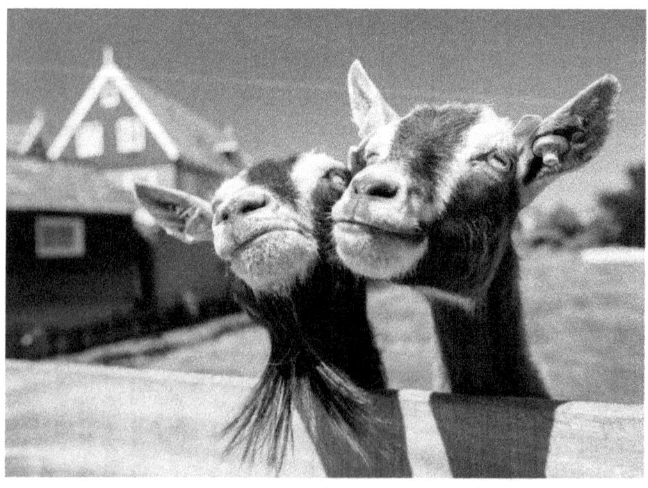

The Rut Period

Seven weeks after birth the male goats can breed. This doesn't mean they should be bred immediately, but it's possible they can make female goats pregnant, or try to jump over any other female goat or sheep. So, when the young goat starts to jump over things or animals, experts say this stage of a goat's life is known as the Rut period. The goat can now breed, and should be treated as a young goat. Male goats which are also known as "bucks" can easily breed any time they want; bucks are always able to breed at any time, they just avoid breeding in weather that is not normal. Bucks avoid breeding in harsh weather such as rain or snow. When female goats are not in heat, they try to avoid the breeding session, and, as a result, bucks will do everything to get their attention. This includes spitting, snorting, and urinating on them to make themselves smellier. They will also drink their urine to increase their own smell. The heat period for female goats is known as Estrus, and they become receptive to mating. After every 21 days the female goats go into heat which lasts about 1-3 days. Many breeds which include Boers, Pygmies and Nigerians can breed all year. The rest breed seasonally which means that they will more likely breed every 21 days in the fall from August to January. Fully grown female goats are good to be bred when they are 8 months old. Experts suggest to breed the females when they reach 1 year. Female goats show signs when they are in heat. They will mount other female goats, jump around, wag their tails, fight, emit clear mucosal discharge from the vagina, or make noises for no apparent reason. The gestation period lasts 5 months. Goat owners often breed their goats one time in a year to vary the milk supply. A female goat can be milked even if she is pregnant, but it is good to let her dry so that her body can rest and recover. A female goat, which is also called a doe, can make babies and give birth all her life. However, pregnancy tends to cause more difficulties as she gets old.

Chapter Summary

- Goats are not a new species. They have been around for many centuries. Goats were first domesticated by the inhabitants who were bounded by the Tigris and Euphrates rivers. They are usually found in areas from Turkmenistan to Turkey.

- Goats belong to the Bovidae family, a broad group which shares significant characteristics with mammals like cows, bison and sheep.

- Domestic goats can be found in harsh environments such as mountains and forests.

- Goats can be bought from other farmers, wholesale markets, Craigslist, breeders websites, and many other sources.

- One should choose a goat based on it's breed, legality, size, health and gender. Your preference must depend on your purpose.

- You can raise goats to earn money; goat meat is extremely healthy and commands good prices.

- In rural areas, mainly villages, goats are released in the morning and are taken to their fences at night. Urban goats are caged.

- Good clean water is the main source of hydration for goats and is very important in maintaining their health.

- It doesn't matter what type of housing it is, but it must be clean, dry and ventilated.

- The Rut period for bucks can create difficulties for the animals and for the owner. The male is always ready, but this doesn't mean the female goat is also ready!

In the next chapter you will learn….

CHAPTER TWO

GETTING YOUR GOAT READY FOR A HOME

Goats are not the first animal that springs to mind when we think of pets. People do not usually prefer them. They can be seen as a rather eccentric choice. For one thing, the resources that are needed to ensure their comfort and happiness are far more complex than those required for relatively ordinary pets such as cats or dogs. They need much more in terms of shelter and accommodation, and need to be kept separate from the human home. A goat can hardly be accommodated in your living room if for no other reason than it's not in their nature to take to being house-broken!

Secondly, their personalities can be odd or stubborn, and, it must be acknowledged, they have habits that can be off-putting; an animal that sometimes urinates on itself - as is the case with male billy goats in the breeding season - isn't necessarily going to appeal to a potential pet-owner, no matter how attractive female goats might think the habit is!

On the other hand, many normal pets demonstrate what we would consider to be unpleasant habits from time to time. They are all part of the animal kingdom, after all. Perhaps it can do us well, as human beings, to remind ourselves occasionally that the world of Nature is not an antiseptic, air-conditioned place.

Set against any less appealing aspects is the fact that goats are intelligent, friendly, affectionate and sensitive creatures. Establish a friendship with a goat, and you will have a loyal companion for as long as it lives. Goats, incidentally, usually have a life-span of 10 to 14 years. Goats can make terrific pets. If you live in the countryside, for example, it's perfectly possible to take your goat out walking or hiking, much in the same way you would a dog. You will very likely find they are better at hiking than you are!

However, a goat as a pet is not for everybody. We will discuss all the things needed to care for and raise a goat in a safe and healthy environment. Goats can be awkward creatures. For example, they want to chew on everything, and this can include your hair and clothes! If you want to get one for yourself, then it's necessary you do the research. Henceforth, you do not need to go anywhere, just keep reading and we will go through all the necessary things.

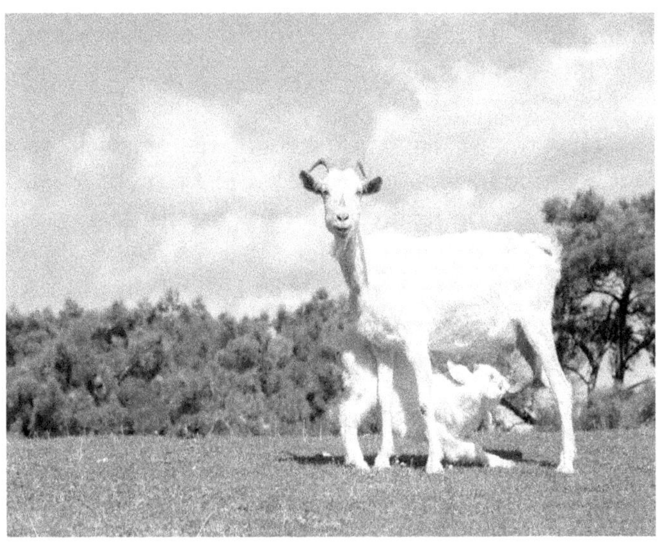

How to Start with Goats

People sometimes have the idea of owning goats, but are apprehensive and not sure where to begin. Goats are both weird and cute animals; put those two qualities together, and you have an animal that is fun to be around. The first thing to consider is fencing. Make sure you have sturdy fencing surrounding your yard. Normal cattle fencing won't do. Goats require special fencing which is used only for these animals. Netting or thermal fencing is also good to prevent them putting their heads through. Sometimes, if they have horns, they will stick them into this netting. Now, to prevent this, it's up to you if you want to disbud your goat or not. This basically means dehorning the goat. This is something new goat owners don't usually want to carry out unless they have someone experienced to do it for them. Be aware this is often a painful process for the animal, and some owners regard it as inhumane.

Then you will have to decide whether you will breed your goats yourself or ask someone else to do it for you. If you do decide to breed them yourself, then, rather obviously, you will have to get a male goat, also known as a buck or billy. Kikos are the best kind in this case. You will also have to build a separate space for them. They are not mean, rude or aggressive, but they are very strong. When you keep your buck separate from your does, that netting or barbed wire won't be good for them. You will have to get something, perhaps welded pipes that will keep them from breaking through. Otherwise, in breeding season, a buck will simply break a normal fence. After organising a fence, you will need to have a clean water supply for them. They also like to drink from a pond or a creek, but they don't like to get wet, so make sure you have a good water supply close to your barn or homestead.

You will also need sufficient housing where you can keep your animals. You don't need to have something extraordinary for them. Use whatever you have to provide them with a dry and warm shelter because they don't like to get wet. When it rains, a cow or a horse will stand in the downpour, but goats will go running until they find a dry spot. So you will need to keep that in mind. Build something that will keep them out of the rain, and from those icy winter winds. You can get some small three-sided structures which can be moved around; these can be placed where there's a dry and clean spot of land.

Also, you will have to decide on their feed. Will you give them grains every day or hay every day? Decide how much pasture you have and can give them. What kinds of hay are you are going to buy? Where will you buy your hay from? Will you feed them hay during the winter season too? A good idea for hay is to check out horse ranches where they have race horses too. Race horses are very picky when it comes to their hay so such ranches will be able to assist you. Alfalfa, or an Alfalfa mixture, is great food for goats, and they will do well on this feed, combined with hay. Another thing is where to get good quality goats from? There are a lot of possibilities online on Facebook, Craigslist, and other sites. If you opt to get registered goats, you will need to pay two times what you'd normally pay. Cross-breeds, on the other hand, will be much cheaper to get.

The next question is how to decide which breed you will have? Which breed will work for you? Where to start? If you are new to this, don't begin with registered animals because they're very expensive. Start with something that doesn't cost you a lot of money. You can start with Pygmy goats. They are excellent for new owners. They are not that expensive, and they make affectionate pets too. People also think it is absolutely necessary to have a livestock guard, when actually this isn't always the case. It really depends on where you live and your surroundings. If you start with one acre of land, sturdy fencing and live in a safe area, you might not need a guard. If you have a larger area for your goats to roam in, and you live in a rural area where there are predators, then you will certainly need one. A dog will make a terrific livestock guard. But remember the dog must have been brought up around goats because he will spend a lot of his time with them, so it's necessary for him to be familiar with their habits, and be friendly towards them. Another option, if you don't want to get a dog, is a donkey. Donkeys are great guardians if you have a huge herd and a large area of land. They can keep the entire Wild at bay.

Things You Need to Know Before Getting Goats

When people want to buy goats, they get a little confused as to what they should or shouldn't do. Some people simply want goats as pets, some want to start a dairy business, and others want to have meat goats. But for all of these different approaches, there are some things that go for every kind of goat, and which you should know beforehand. Firstly, they are a lot easier to look after when compared to some other big animals such as cows or buffaloes. Secondly, they are a great way to begin when you want to go for something small. They are small animals so they don't take up a lot of space.

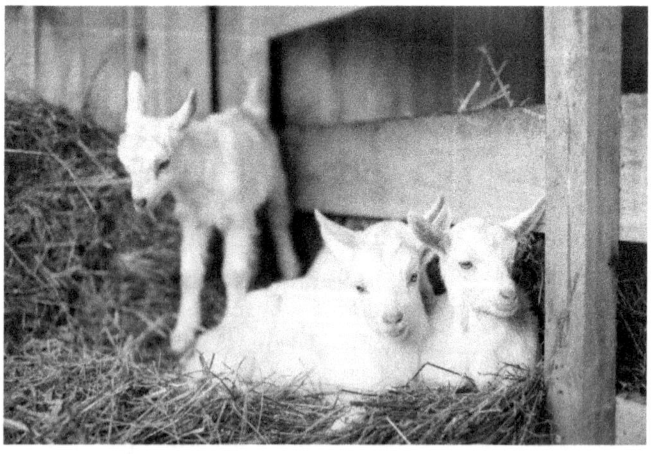

You will also need to do the fencing beforehand. Because fencing used for other cattle won't be able to keep goats in. They tend to jump a lot and will test its strength, so barbed wire or 4-inch square fencing will work perfectly. 36 inches to 40 inches in height is perfect for them. Goats are somewhat weird animals, so while setting up a fence for them, remember this saying; "If it won't hold water, it won't hold goats." This might seem a slight exaggeration, but it does give you an idea of the safeguards you should take. Another thing is that goats always want to go to where it's dry. It doesn't depend on the temperature. Whether it is winter, summer, fall or spring they don't like to get wet. So you will need to have a place where they can go to keep themselves dry and free from any draft.

You may also want to have a livestock guardian. Goats are small animals and they can easily become targets of bobcats, coyotes, and other wild animals, so the last thing you want is to invest your money into them, and experience the disaster of losing them to these hunters. Especially during the kidding season, when you have kids roaming here and there, it is pretty easily for other predatory animals to attack and kill them. When you live in a rural area, and have some wild animals around you, this becomes a necessity. You will also need to remember; don't buy just one goat. They are herd animals and they get very depressed when they are lonely. New goat owners don't take this seriously, and sometimes they just have to bear the worst consequences. Also, you will have your own needs and purposes, and you will acquire your goats according to those needs. There are many dairy breeds out there. If you want to get a lot of milk, or if you want to make butter, there are separate breeds for these purposes, so you will need to do your research in this area. Goats are a lot of fun to have around, and you will learn many things around them. All you need to do is make sure you thoroughly research before embarking on becoming an owner.

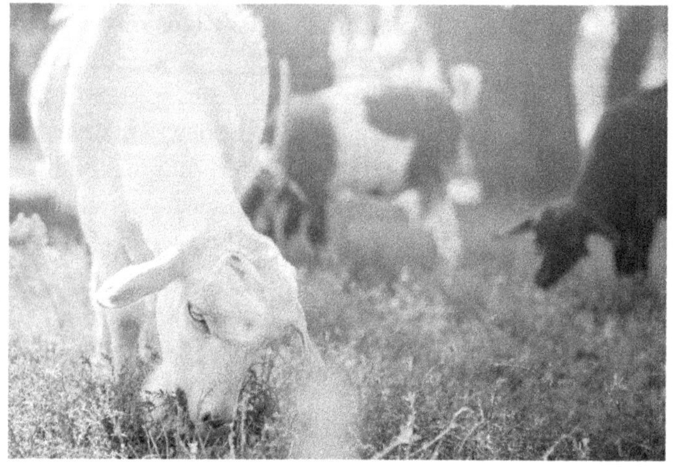

What Kind of Breed Is Ideal as a Pet?

The first and foremost thing to do is to find out whether it is legal to keep farm animals in residential areas in your country. They are illegal in certain states. Some neighbourhoods also forbid certain kinds of animals as pets. After you have understood the rules governing where you live, you can decide on which breed you want to get.

Billy Goats are not recommended as they stink, are pretty aggressive and actually urinate on themselves. Wethers are male goats that were castrated when young;

these are much more even-tempered, and more suitable as pets. Norwegian Dwarf Goats or Pygmy Goats make great pets, as they are small and easy to look after. The major difference between the two is that, though they both are small, Norwegian Dwarf Goats are bred for milk production, whereas Pygmy goats are stockier and raised for meat.

What Age is Ideal for Adoption?

When adopting, it is recommended to get them as babies and bottle feed them. They will get more attached to you this way. For bottle feeding, it is recommended to get a week old baby; he would have enough of his mother's milk for proper nourishment; this mother's milk contains colostrum which is simply a fluid that many mammals, including goats, produce from their breasts when nursing. It is extremely nutritious. You can also get four to six weeks old babies if you want a grown one. Moreover, it is important to decide whether to get a male or a female. You can get a female or a male, or both males. Be aware though, that females are a little pricey compared to the males. Also, give each goat a proper name and call them by that name. They will learn to respond to it. This helps in the process of bonding between animal and owner.

How to Feed a Baby Goat?

Bottle feeding your baby goat should be done with care. You would need a baby bottle, a kid nipple, goat replacement milk, and colostrum replacement. It requires practice. It is actually quite easy, but when done wrong, your goat might get sick or eventually die. Cow's milk is not recommended for bottle feeding. Baby goats need to be well trained to adapt to the bottle feeding process.

Babies are required to be fed four times a day in the first month. However, as they grow you can reduce it to three times. You can also give them hay or little amounts of grain to help with their rumen development. However, too much hay, too early, would cause digestive problems. Clean and fresh water, along with pasture and hay, could be given regularly after the baby gets 30 days old. The amount of milk can be gradually decreased when your baby goat starts eating like an adult goat. You should also contact your veterinarian for further tips and monthly checkup regarding nourishment of your baby goat.

How to Feed an Adult Goat?

An adult goat largely feeds on hay, grains and grass. 80% of their food is dry hay. It does not have to be expensive because they will eat the hay that is the cheapest. Go for the cheapest and driest hay out there. It saves money and does wonders for the goat too. They also love some vegetables and their peels. Give them a banana or two. The South Asian breeds are often fed with a special drink to cleanse their stomach. It's water and flour in a ratio of 3:1 respectively. The farmers and cattle herders have suggested this drink as a tonic when their goats are having digestion issues.

In winter, they need a special caring and feeding routine. They usually eat dry hay, and you can mix it with Alfalfa, or you can just get horse hay. These are usually available in bales, but before buying you must check, by taking it a little apart, that it is good quality hay. When you see there is no mold or wetness inside, then that usually indicates it's good quality hay. For treats, you can get them rolled oats. They love this particular food. They will also enjoy a mixture of some corns, barley and oats. Some recipes also have molasses mixed in to provide sweetness. They absolutely love this mixture, but, of course, you don't want to give them too much. A handful or two would be enough for one time because these are basically all grains; this will swell them up and they will start bloating. Another thing to remember is to keep them separate from other animals at meal times; they love exploring and they will want to eat their food. They love chickens' feed and they will eat it until they bloat. This will be dangerous for them, and they might die. They won't be able to regurgitate it as it is all granular. You can also get a tray where you can pop in some bales of hay. That tray will minimize your waste of hay. You will obviously not be completely able to stop it but it will work fairly well.

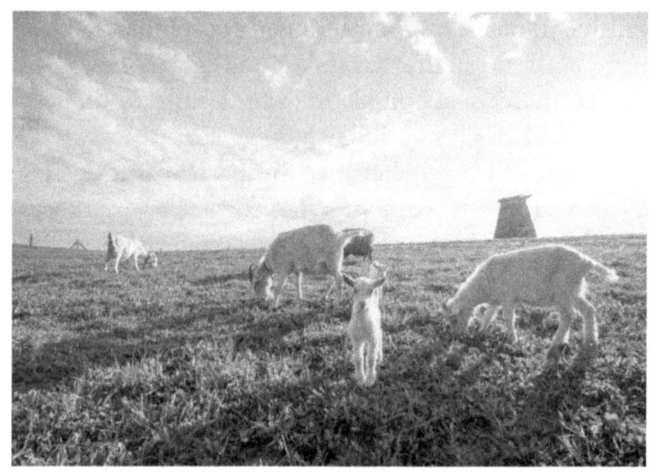

You can give them grains, but in limited quantity, or they will start bloating. They also pasture on grass wherever they see it. Like many grazing animals, they require food all the time, so hay must always be present. Clean and fresh water in a small bucket or trough is also necessary. If your goats are small, you must make sure they can reach the low water level in their trough. It's a sad sight to see a trough where the water isn't high enough for the goat to drink.

How to Provide your Goat a Proper Shelter?

Baby Goat

Baby goats require a clean, dry, warm and draft-free shelter with bedding for their comfort. Hay and dry grass is very suitable to spread and cover the ground. Soiled and urinated bedding should be replaced by new bedding regularly.

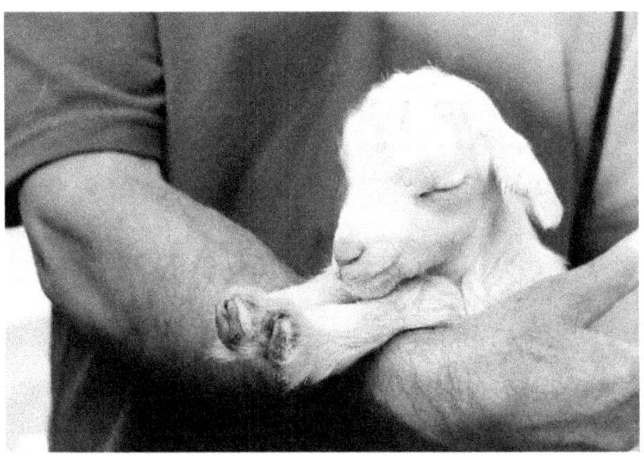

Young Goats

Young goats also need proper bedding with warm, draft-free, sheltered space. Layers of dry hay must be spread on the ground for their comfort. Their bedding area must be cleaned every day. Wet and soiled hay must be replaced by fresh and dry material. You can also use uneaten or leftover hay to save your money.

Goats Also Need a Yard

The yard needn't be big; just somewhere they can run around, and play and move freely. If you have a garden with flowers and grass, you need to keep it separated because they will eat everything. Goats love climbing, so you will need to place some bumpy steps for their jumping and playing.

You will need a fencing area for your goats to keep them away from your garden. If you have small goats, then a four feet high fence is just about right, but if you have taller goats then five to six feet high fence is recommended. This is a must to prevent them from jumping over and running away. Also, don't place anything near that boundary or your goat will climb it and jump over.

How to Take Care of Goats?

Goats should be vaccinated according to your veterinarian's advice to prevent possible illnesses. Usually goats are resistant to many diseases, but bacterial fungus, fever or indigestion is very common among them. If you see signs like laziness or low appetite, then take them to a veterinarian immediately.

Their hooves need to be trimmed, but it should be done by an expert or they will catch fungus or bacteria. You can bathe them once a week or a fortnight. A huge brush to remove all the knots and fleas should also be used once or twice a week, but they would be absolutely fine without it. Taking them hiking or walking with you will help their digestive system.

How to do the Fencing?

You can do short-term fencing as well as long-term fencing. It depends upon the type of animal you have. Short-term fencing can be done using a wire, poly tape, or electric netting. It is usually meant to keep stray animals away. Sometimes children also trouble these animals, so this way they would also keep their distance. You can also use high-tensile wire, if your neighbourhood is a little unsafe, to keep potential culprits at bay.

Long-term fencing is done to secure the boundary altogether. You can use wood panels either in a vertical arrangement, or horizontal long panels would also do the job. This fencing has to be at least four feet high to prevent your goats from jumping over. Woven wire fencing is the best. It will keep hunters at a safe distance.

High tensile electric wires, or barbed wire, can also be a great option to make the fencing more effective. However, it is important to remember not to use anything that would harm your goat. Also, do not keep any space where your goat can put their head through. It may get stuck, and in case of wires, they will lacerate their heads. In addition, goats chew on everything, so they will nibble on the lock of the fence, and if it is not properly locked, they will open it and run.

How to Keep Your Goat Safe?

Choose the Proper Fencing:

Goats are curious, persistent, and resourceful animals. That in itself is a good reason for you to choose their fencing wisely. While choosing the fencing, make sure you get 4-inch square ones. They are ideal as your goats won't be able to pass its head through that smaller space. A 6-inch square fencing is not recommended because your goat will pass their head through and it could get trapped. The fencing should be at least 4-feet high attached to 7-feet wooden poles.

Place a Ramp in the Water Trough:

Goats love jumping on to or over anything they find. The same goes for baby goats too, and while drinking water, they will jump into the trough. Since they are small, they won't know how to jump back out. So, for their safety, place a ramp inside the water trough so their feet would find purchase on to something, and they would be able to safely climb out. Also, keep a separate trough for baby goats because, even though they are nursing, they will still need water to drink.

Fencing Must be Secured

Strong and sturdy fencing would make sure no one would enter in your does' yard and harm them.

Keep Small Water Troughs around Baby Goats

Use smaller water troughs for your baby goats. Huge buckets with high water levels are dangerous for them. They feet are not mature enough; they won't know how to come out if they jump into them. Their chances of drowning are very high.

Keep the Handle of the Bucket Flat

Goats are very curious animals. They nibble on everything so when you use water buckets, make sure its handle is flat. Especially around baby goats, because if the handle is in a vertical position, then the baby goat might get its head stuck while drinking. It would be hard for them to untangle, and they might injure or break their neck in the process.

Baby Goats Must be Placed Safely

As with most species, babies are the easiest of prey. If you have baby goats, make sure you keep them in your peripheral vision. Do not let them stray too far. Keep them in very secured sections. Sometimes people steal them too, so it is recommended to keep them near you.

Lock the Fence at Night

Keep the fence locked at night since this is frequently when predators are at work. The fencing should also be locked from the inside. It should also be high enough to keep those predators from jumping inside.

Chapter Summary

- When you decide to purchase a goat for your farm or your homestead, you must research thoroughly about everything related to them before actually going to buy one.

- Goats are herd animals and they are very social, so always buy two goats or they get lonely and depressed.

- Kikos are preferred if you want to have male goats. Boer goats and Pygmy goats are good meat producers. Nigerian Dwarf goats are good milk breeders.

- You must decide on the type of breed. Then you can purchase it from a local breeder. Or check your local farmers' market where goat cheese and soap sellers will be able to guide you.

- When getting a baby goat, the ideal age is 2 weeks, because by then, the baby would have nursed their mother's milk with colostrum, which is very important for their immune system.

- You can also get a 4 weeks old baby, and by then, they don't need any bottle feeding. To bottle feed your baby goat, you will need a bottle with a cub nipple and milk with colostrum so that it can be substituted for their mother's milk.

- Baby goats need to be milk fed 3 to 4 times a day, which can be reduced when they get to 4 weeks old. You can then add dry hay and grains along with that.

- Goats' natural food is hay, grass and grains. They will grow very healthy on that diet, but the owner must not overfeed them, or the goat will start to have digestive problems and other issues. Dry hay doesn't have to be expensive.

- A proper warm shelter, with dry hay bedding, enough space for them to move freely, and some things to jump upon, is necessary for both baby and adult goats. Don't keep those things near the fence or they will jump over it.

- Fencing must be at least 4 feet high and attached with 5 to 6 feet of vertical poles. If you have taller goats, then 5 feet is recommended.

- Go for proper 4-inch square fencing which is especially for goats, because it will stop them hurting themselves. You can also have both short term and long term fencing.

- Short-term is temporary to keep all the predators, like wild dogs, coyotes, foxes, at bay. Long term fencing is used to keep your animals from straying far.

- Goats also need grooming periodically. This includes proper bathing, shearing or clipping, and trimming their hooves. Hoof trimming should be done by an expert.

- Proper vaccinations should also be done, as guided by your vet, to prevent all kinds of diseases, internal worms, and other signs of unhealthiness.

- To keep your goats safe, you must secure them safely at night, especially baby goats because they are easy prey.

- Small water troughs should be placed for them. Keep the handle of buckets flat so baby goats won't stick their head through. Keep the fencing secured.

In the next chapter you will learn….

CHAPTER THREE

HANDLING YOUR GOAT WITH CARE

Once you have purchased the right quality goat for yourself, the question rises of how to handle your goat with care? There are certain basic tips and tricks to handle them which will hopefully make your life stress-free as well as your animals. Obviously, every animal doesn't act the exact same way, but again some basics and fundamentals would make your life a little easier. There are certain behavioral principles associated with goats, so focusing on them, and acting accordingly, does help.

Why is it Necessary to Handle Them with Care?

Animals need love and care like any other living thing. It helps them to grow and thrive. Many people believe that even plants need you to talk to them in order to be healthy. Goats, as is the way of many domestic creatures, naturally become warm and friendly with their owner when they receive attention from them. You have to be good at handling them with care because it will help them increase in their ability to perform well. This will automatically increase their milk and meat production, and it will reduce the chances of injuries and illnesses. But, obviously, you will first need to understand the natural behavior and instinctive reactions of your goats. Henceforth, armed with this knowledge, you will be able to handle those reactions with control, and work in a smarter way to your best advantage.

Aggressive Behavior by the Handler Would Not Work

You must appreciate that your goat is not the same as a sheep. Handling a goat is completely different from handling a sheep. People make this mistake a lot, and expect their goat to react the same way a sheep does. This will not happen. Goats don't meet situations the way humans do. Goats are the animals of prey, and humans are the hunters, so yelling, screaming, rapid movement, getting too close to them, and other aggressive behavior from the human side, should be avoided. That, in turn, will help reduce the stress goats can cause humans.

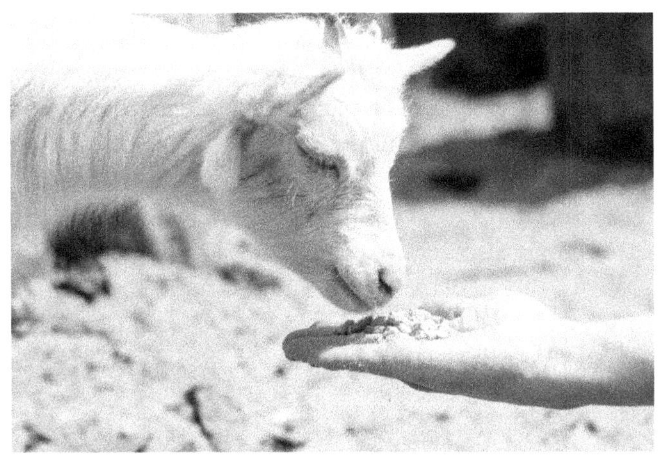

Goats are curious and social animals. They want to go anywhere or everywhere, and that is why they are the easiest of prey, and very prone to being hurt. But they are very independent too, so if a goat chooses to stray away from its herd, then it is fine, but the handler must make sure that it should not be forced to do so; otherwise it will panic and get stressed. In addition, goats are herd animals and move in family groups. Whenever they graze, they are always led by a presiding female, also known as the flock queen. The queen is responsible for leading the group to where there is food or water, and no immediate threats. The queen will initiate this, so the handler must motivate the flock queen to continue with its venture. This generally happens when you have more than seven goats to make a herd. If you own a single or a pair, the animal would want to graze alone.

While grazing, goats tend to scatter, so it is difficult to keep the herd in one place. For example, when there is a threat, the handler would obviously want to herd all the goats together, but they may well scatter and turn to face their attacker. They might try to challenge their attacker by charging towards it because they are usually not the type of animal to back away or flee. In addition, when goats get frightened, they whine, sneeze, and stomp their feet. In case of younger goats, they usually freeze in one place so their attacker doesn't notice them. Scared goats also tend to sulk, pack in one corner, and lie down.

Herd and Drive Them Together Using Their Intelligence

But goats are extremely intelligent animals so, to avoid this problem of scattering in a pasture, the handler can use food to drive them all together. In case of the above described scenarios, a food bucket or something that the handler used to train the herd, will draw them back into the pack, and move them in a direction away from the threat. It is similar to how a dog reacts to a bone thrown at him. When the threat is near, the handler must know multiple ways to handle the herd and keep all the goats safe, because they will panic, and if not handled with care and presence of mind, they will hurt each other and themselves. Using their natural intelligence would give the handler an upper hand, and would make it a lot easier for making them react to the tactic he employs. If they are taught to run with their handler, they will follow at the time of need. Also, the handler can make them learn commands using ticking technique, and it would serve effectively in times of emergency. One can also use a dog guardian to look for these threats, and help the handler to deal with them.

Use Their Visual Range to Your Benefit

Goats have a visual range between 320 to 360 degrees, and they use this vision to keep an eye out for potential threats, and to keep track of their herd. The handler must use this vision as a stimulus to move the goat. Visual stimuli are the most efficient way of moving the animals. Also, this visual pressure helps activate their fright and flight reaction. The handler can use this technique to move them away from him, but their flight reaction would work when the handler is in the animal's line of vision, or shall we say, its personal space. Goats are not easy to move, because they don't tend to move willingly, and extra pressure is stressful for them. Natural instincts are much easier to work with, and this way you won't have to work harder with your goats because you know their strengths. Working with that will give you your desired results earlier than it would have in other circumstances.

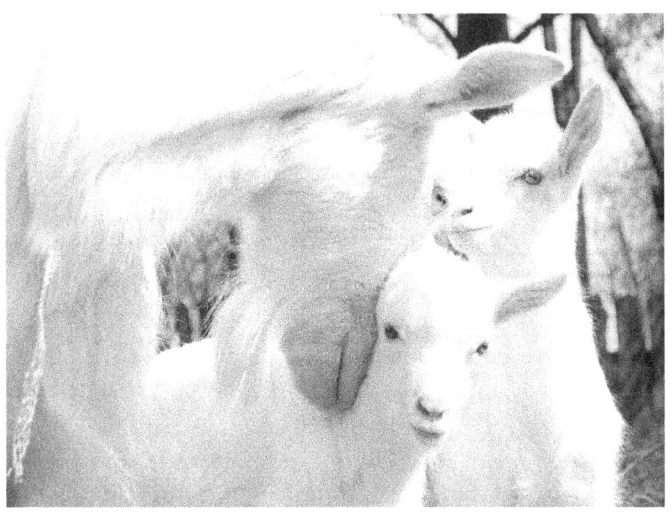

Patience Will Take You a Long Way

The facilities where goats are kept must be free of holes for them to go through or climb in. When you want to move your animals from one place to another, it can happen that it's difficult to load them on the vehicle. To avoid this, give them some time to get used to their surroundings, and they will be easier to move. The same goes for new barns, farms, yards, or any other place you want to take or move them to. Patience is a virtue and exercising it will reward you. It will reduce stress on both sides. It goes best with handling all animals. Goats have the ability to sense their handler's impatience, and will likely behave disobediently. Any kind of pressure to make them run or move a little quicker will panic them and they will react by missing their track, or missing the gate they were supposed to get through. Remind yourself that, sometimes if you have an hour to move them, it will take only 15 minutes, yet other times it would be quite the opposite; you will have only 15 minutes, but it will take a whole hour to move them.

Some Quick Tips

Handle your goat using its natural instincts. Don't act like a predator in handling them, don't get impatient or angry, and definitely don't hit them. Don't try to herd or move a lot of animals at the same time; this could easily create chaos and confusion. Handle them from behind by using slow movements, and keep your patience. Keep yourself safe too while handling them because some goats do charge and butt, so try to be extra careful around them. When they do so, you will need to know how to gently tell them you will not allow this behavior. Also, goats don't like to be pulled by their collars. It annoys them, so put a leash on them to move them. Be aware that goats will try to eat almost anything so, if you value your beautiful flower bed, keep it fenced off from them!

Handling Pregnant Goats

There is a breeding season, and kidding season, and in between there is the gestation period. In that period there is quite some work for the handler. All the goats should get their shots in this timeframe. Babies grow mostly in the last two months, so the handler must watch the animals' food closely during those months. Also, if the goat is a freshener - in other words if it's her first time getting pregnant - then the handler has to make her comfortable on the milking stand because they get a little fidgety and jumpy.

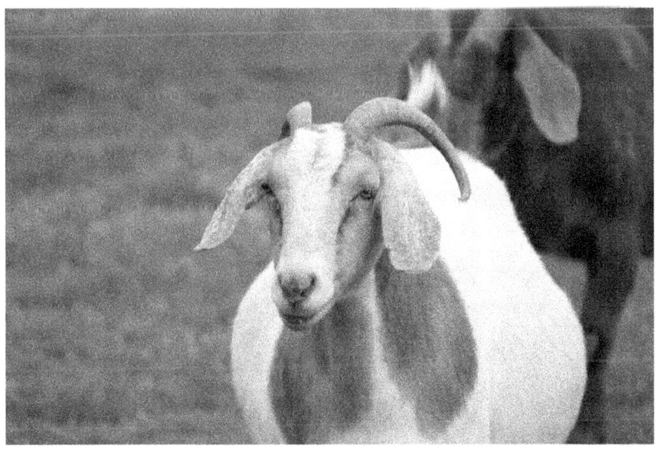

Handling New-Born Babies

There are some basics to remember here. Babies, when they come out of their mother's body, are very weak and small. They cannot look out for themselves. Therefore, the first thing the handler must do is keep them warm because cold could kill them. Then the baby should be provided milk as soon as possible for all the important nutrition, so that they can have the strength to get up, walk to their mother, nurse themselves, or take the bottle feed that you give them. Also, if you have a farm or homestead and kidding outside, you must make sure the conditions are right for the mother. Always protect them from hypothermia .

Flipping Your Goat

When you take care of your goats and handle them, there are a few who are a little uncooperative and stubborn. Handling them is a bit of a challenge because the size alone would level you on the ground, and do you quite some damage.

If your goat has horns, make sure you caress them, and pat them from the side. The neck of the animal must be at your side so they won't be able to use their horns.

But if your young baby goat comes at you using their horns in an aggressive way, this may be to test how you react. You must stop them immediately. What you can do is yell 'NO', very loudly. Also, you can gesture openly and scare them. This will stop them. But if this happens again, you can flip the goat. You have to be really careful as it is a very offensive move, disruptive to the animal, and will take some time for them to trust you again. Flipping means you reach under them, grab their legs using both hands, pull it towards your chest, and flip them over. Make sure you are gentle. Then you will stand over them, between their front and hind legs, hold their front legs and say 'NO'. This will show them that you are the handler, you're in charge, and this kind of behavior isn't acceptable. But make sure you only do that as a last resort, when they misbehave or hit you again and again. Now, once you've flipped them, take your time, and they will get calm and submissive. Then you tell them it is okay. You pat and caress them so they know you still love them.

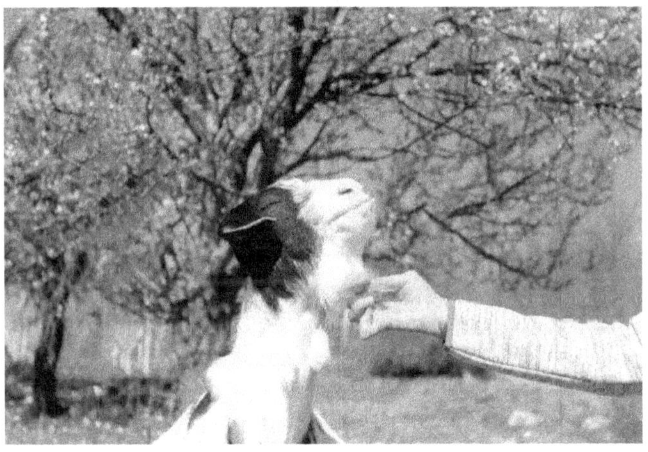

Flipping a big goat of around 200 pounds sounds quite a challenge, and requires a whole lot of techniques. Nonetheless, when you do it right it is quite simple. You will grab one front and one hind leg, pull them against you, and push your chest onto them; your weight will help you flip them over. Then you will stand over them, and pin their shoulders by keeping your feet a little tight around their shoulders. Again, don't hurt them. You will speak to them, they will submit, and you will let them get up on their legs. Then caress them to show your love for them.

Training Your Goat

You can train your goats for a number of things. Goats are smart animals, but you will need to be very patient; it will take a lot of time and repetitive training to get them to understand what it is that you want from them. Training your goats would help reduce the stress when the thing is actually needed to be done. But you must not lose your patience. Don't push them or hit them to try and make them do what you want. Don't force them to do your bidding. This could break the bond between you and your animal. Slowly and gradually, they will learn to do things, and will cooperate with you.

Some Goat Treats While Training

It is important to train your goats, and they will cooperate with you more if you provide them with treats when they do well. You can train more than one goat at a time. Try to know beforehand what your goat loves most and treat them accordingly. Animals usually do anything if the reward involves food. There are some things that goats really like: carrots, animal crackers, vegetable peels, apples, almonds, grains, flatbreads, etc.

Milk Stand Training

It is also good to train your goat for the milk stand. This is beneficial, not only for milk, but for the animal as well. So, what you will do, you will need to make your goat stand on the milk-stand. Then you must pat them, and make them feel like everything is okay so they don't feel nervous. Now, you will need to put their head through the stand's front gap. Make sure their gap is enough for their head, and ensure you don't hurt them. Again, you will make them feel it is completely okay if they are being held still because you're not going to hurt them. Then you will pat them gently, and touch the udders. Your goat might not be used to it, so they will get jumpy, but you will also keep reminding them that you will not hurt them. Then lift their legs one at a time. Then let them go. If you discover that the goat is very agitated and won't cooperate then take a break and try again later. Don't force the animal, and, perhaps just as importantly, don't force yourself. You can repeat this process twice a week. It will take time, but your goat will get used to it. Then when kidding time comes near, take them up on the stand regularly. You can also lure them with treats if they won't cooperate in getting easily on the stand. An option you might want to try is using goat hobbles. These are canvas straps which fasten just above the goats knees and will prevent the goat from kicking.

Train to be Led or Leashed

There are two kinds of goats. There is one that likes to be dragged, and there is the one that will drag you with them. When training goats, you will need to be very gentle and patient with them. They are smart learners, and your patience will reward you. People pull goats while on a leash. This is not the method to do so. When you pull them, they in turn will pull against you very strongly, and will drag you along. The correct way is to move the leash sideways, then pull, and they will come along with you. It's best, normally, to use leashes with goats that have a collar; you really don't want to be tying a leash directly to the animal's neck because this creates the possible danger of choking.

Some goats don't like to pull, and you will need to drag them in order to train them. What you can do is wrap the cord around the front of your body and walk using the strength of it. They will give you a hard time. What you can do is drag them, pull sideways, turn in a circle, and pull them again. This will frustrate your goat and they will have no choice but to come with you because you will not give up. That is how you train a goat who needs to be dragged.

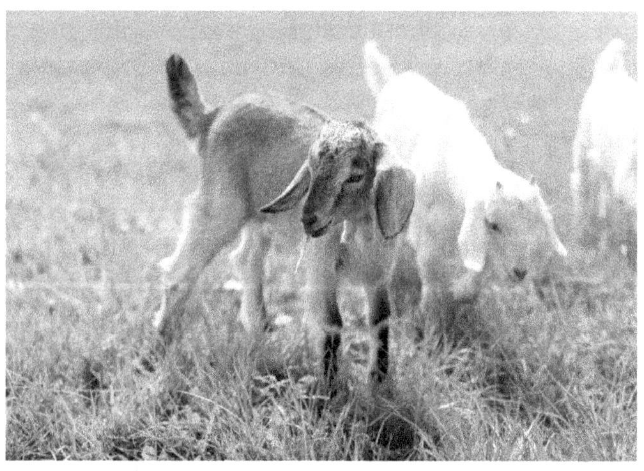

Some goats like to be in the lead, and will pull you along with them. It is usually not liked by the handler. So what do you do? As soon as they get ahead of you, turn around so that now you are in the lead. In this way, you train them to not pull you or misbehave when on a leash.

It is easier to turn a goat then to pull one. Whenever you get a goat and they don't cooperate, the fastest way to train them is to tie them with a leash to a fence. They will struggle, but eventually will discover that it won't budge. Give them food there. They will start respecting their leash from this training. Baby goats can also be trained this way.

Training on Electric Fence

Electric fencing is for the safety of your animals so obviously you will need to train goats to stay away from them. One thing you need to bear in mind is the importance of getting someone else to help you with this training. It can't be done alone, so get yourself a training partner. When you start training, and when the goat goes toward the fencing, it is their nose which will be zapped first. This is a good thing because it is not life threatening, and they should react by running in the opposite direction. However, with younger babies, the possibility exists they will panic and run forward. If you have 6-inch fencing, then they will get stuck, and will be zapped continuously, which is fatal. That's why having a partner will pay off, since they will see the danger, and immediately close down the entire electric system.

Your goat will understand the electric fencing when they experience a zap or two, but it has to be on their own terms. Don't push them into it, don't force them, take your time and let them take theirs. If you attempt to physically force them into experiencing the zap they will think it's just something you're inflicting on them rather than their discovering it's something they have caused themselves by deciding to go near the fence. A point to bear in mind is that the goat will need to be zapped on their nose, as it is the most sensitive part. Anywhere else on the body will not bring the desired result. Not every goat needs to get a shock to learn to avoid the fence. Some may not require any shocks at all if they prefer to remain with the herd. Goats are smart creatures and, if they see one of the herd experiencing a shock from an electrified fence, they may well realize they should stay away from it themselves. However, inevitably there are some stubborn goats who will need more than one or two shocks. It is only a tiny sting so it won't do any permanent damage, and the sting goes away as soon as you shut down the system.

Trim your fencing line to avoid all damage to your animals, and keep checking every now and then that the current flows smoothly throughout the fence. Training them as a pack would help a great deal. They tend to learn by seeing each other, so this would be more than enough to keep them away from the fencing. Sometimes luring does the work too. It may seem a little unfair, but it will let you know whether the goat is trained or not. Station someone beyond the line with some treats, and see how the goats react.

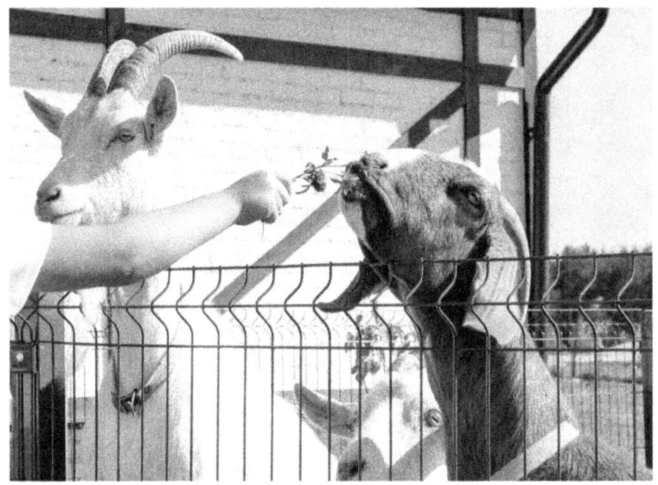

You can train goats using clicker tricks. You can make them jump onto your lap, perform funny tricks, and how to walk or perform for a show. Potty training usually doesn't work with goats. It is not in their natural behavior to be litter box trained, so they will go wherever they like. The last thing and the most important thing to remember is that patience is key in all of this. Take all the time your goat wants, and the end result will be very good.

Chapter Summary

- Handling your goat with care is very important if you want your goat to give you the results you want. They have some basic traits, which helps you as well as your animal.
- Aggressive behavior from the handler would do no good. Yelling, screaming, pushing and pulling, would not only stress you but also your animals, and that would not bring any desirable results for you.
- Goats are intelligent animals; when you keep your patience it becomes easy to train and handle them. Using that intelligence to your advantage would make things more fun and easy.
- When the handler takes the herd for grazing, handling them with food would make it uncomplicated and, even in the presence of a threat, they would obey.
- Goats have a visual range between 320 to 360 degrees. Using their visual range, and fright and flight technique to move them away from any threat and go anywhere with their handler, would help a great deal in keeping a herd together.
- To make your goats learn anything, and during handling, patience is the key. Repetitive attempts and a lot of waiting would eventually bring good results for the handler, but frustration and

annoyance will not help, and your goats would not cooperate either.

- Don't act like predators. Hitting them would not bring you any advantage.

- When you have any pregnant goat, then it is imperative for the owner to treat them with care. The last two months require a lot more supervision because they need more food, and the owner must make them comfortable where they will give birth.

- Kidding process is also very hard for the doe, so a secluded space is necessary.

- Newborn babies also require close observation and immediate care soon after the delivery.

- When your goat gets a little uncooperative such as jumping on you, or starts butting, or pushing you for no apparent reason, then you can flip them gently, and stand over them so that they realize you will not allow this behavior. This will make them submissive.

- Training them on a milk stand twice a week will make your goat know that you won't harm them, and they will cooperate with you when the time comes.

- When you train your goats, some indulgence in the form of treats when they do well encourages them to be helpful and easy going.

- Goats love almonds, carrots, vegetable peel, and flatbreads, so you can use these to lure them.

- Training on a leash can get a little tricky because some goats don't like to be pulled, and some like to drag the owner. In this case, moving them sideways always does the job instead of pulling and pushing them.

- They will also need training on electric fencing, and this training requires two individuals.

In the next chapter you will learn…

CHAPTER FOUR

HEALTH AND WELLBEING OF A GOAT

There are additional ways to guarantee the health and well-being of a goat, and these methods are as important as food, shelter and a safe environment. We call it grooming, which includes proper bathing, clipping, shearing, brushing and similar acts. Whether you have goats as pets, or for your farming dreams, you will not want them to get sick, catch infections, or have fleas or bugs in their fur. You will want them to be active, pretty, with an ample amount of good quality milk. So, you will need to do some extra steps for their care in this area.

It will also help create a bond between you and your animal, and you will also be able to observe them closely, and see if they are doing fine or not. Consistent and well-organized grooming will ensure your goat remains fit, healthy and active.

Bathing, Brushing and Clipping

Grooming your animal starts with this main step, where you will need to give your goat a proper bath, with brushing and necessary clipping. You will also need proper supplies for the grooming; this includes trimmers, brushes, shampoo, and soap for bathing.

Brushing Your Goat

First of all, you will need all the related supplies for brushing and these include a curry comb and a soft brush. A curry comb is a circular comb, and it comes with a strap where you can slide your hand under it and use it. Use the curry comb in circular movements on the back, sides, abdomen, legs, neck and chest. This is, in effect, a way of massaging the goat, and is very beneficial. Once you've finished that, take the soft brush, and glide it over, working from the animal's neck, in the direction of the coat, then at the sides, rear, legs, abdomen, and gently on the face and ears. You will discover that goats love brushing.

Brushing also helps to increase the blood flow, helps remove all the dead hair, dandruff, and parasitical insects if they have any. It also helps to make sure your goat is free from all potential diseases and injuries, since the skin under the fur would show any blisters, lumps, or broken skin. Brushing could be done periodically, except for their feeding time. It works especially well before bathing your goat.

Bathing Your Goat

Bathing your goat every so often is necessary as it will help to clean all the dirt from their coat. It eliminates lice, and also makes the clipping part very easy. Try not to bathe them quite so often in winter because they may catch a cold. Also, goats don't really like bathing, so you will need to tie them up with a leash to a fence or a tree, or you can make them stand on the milking-stand so they won't be able to budge.

The process is pretty simple. You will need liquid soap for animals. The water should be warm rather than hot. Start by wetting them thoroughly from their face to their rear and legs. Lather them up using soap and scrub gently with your hands, making sure soap doesn't get into their eyes. Scrub each and every part and then rinse. Dry them with a towel, and put them in the sunshine to warm up.

Clipping Your Goat

Clipping your goat half-yearly helps to keep them cool, free of dirt, and keeps away lice, fleas, and other insects. Short hair helps them to keep cool in summer, whereas long hair helps them to stay warm in winter. You will need sharp clippers to avoid hurting them, and if you use electrical ones, check they don't get too hot or it will burn their skin. Also, make sure you know the hair length beforehand, otherwise they will get kind of bald, and they will burn very easily when exposed to strong sunshine. When shaving, go against the hair flow in the opposite direction, and it's best to make them stand on a milk stand.

There are two important areas that need clipping very often. Firstly, the area around the udders, and the tail area before and after kidding. Clip the hair around the udders so that hair won't go into the milk. You will notice that, before and after kidding, fluids and blood get stuck around the vulva and tail portion; you will need to clip the hair around the tail end, the sides, and make it a little brush. Also the underside of the back legs and the vulva need clipping too.

Trimming Your Goat's Hooves

Trimming the hooves is important on a regular basis. Animals are always on their feet, and therefore they require regular observation. While trimming, make sure there are no rocks stuck, and remove any such objects if you see any. Sniff for foul odors because it tells you of rotten hooves. This should be done every two months. Trimming the hooves helps in long-term health, and helps to keep your goat fit and active.

How to Trim Your Goat's Hooves?

Hoof trimming is actually done when the goat's hoof over-grows. It depends on the diet too. A good diet means more hoof over-growing, and it also depends on their breeds. Trimming needs to be done at least four times a year, but you may need to do it more frequently than that, depending on your goat and the type of area you live in. If your goats move more on the mountains and rocks, then their feet will remain in good shape because these surfaces help to wear their hooves off. On the other hand, where there is too much rain, greenery and thick sand, they need more trimming because their hooves don't wear off themselves. You can use hoof trimmers, horse nippers, hoof knives or pocket knives.

Use a trimmer to remove the dirt, and you will see the white soft spongy area in the center where there is blood flow. Obviously don't hurt that part. Trim the sole area around the edges and you will start seeing a white hard part. Cut it up until that part. Remove the dirt from the heel area, and you will be done. This will help them in stable walking, and prevent them from limping. But again, if you're not sure, don't go around experimenting in this area because you may end up doing some permanent damage. An expert's help is recommended.

Daily Exercises for Your Goat

Goats are always on the move, and that pretty much provides for their daily walks and running. But if you don't have a huge yard, or your homestead is small, then you'll still need to exercise your goat on a daily basis. It will keep them active and healthy, their blood circulation will be good, milk production will be good and of fine quality. Moreover, the change of air, along with some funny running and other tricks, also creates a bond between you and the animal. If you have a small pack, then it will become even more of a fun and amazing experience, not only for you, but for your goats. Hard and fast running helps a lot in burning fat and keeping them fit. There are quite a number of exercises you can get your goats to do.

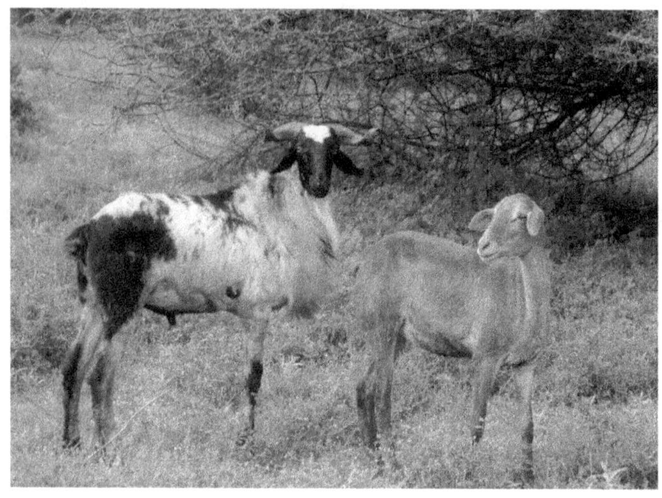

You can make them run laps on a track or in a group. You might have a dog watch over them. He will run after them to make sure they complete their round, and you can tell him when to stop. When he stops, so will your goats.

You can also place some things in your yard for your goats, so they can jump over them. But make sure you do not place it anyway near the fence or they will use it to help them jump right over the fence too.

If you live near mountains or forests, then you can take them walking or hiking with you every day. If your yard is big enough you can make them run there too. It will be very good if you do those exercises with them. They will follow you while running or walking or doing laps. You will enjoy it, and your goats will trust you more, and this will help create a bond. The idea is whatever space is available to you, make use of it. You will not need any special arrangements as they are animals and will do great in the open.

If you want to prepare your goat for a show, then your goat will need exercise to show their competitiveness. You can use treadmills, chariots, and other tricks. Don't overwork them, and pay attention when they need to stop. While doing exercises, if your goat starts panting, then you must call it a day. Afterwards, feed them properly so they will be healthy and active for their next endeavour.

Signs of an Unhealthy Goat

After bringing your goats home, providing them food, proper shelter and other facilities, you must also keep a close eye on your goats to see if they are doing fine or not. Goats are hard and resilient animals, and they don't become sick easily, but you must remain vigilant. Goats seldom sit in one place for long, and you will see them running around, and nibbling things out of curiosity. Thus, the chances are high they will fall ill at some point. Whether your goats are for milk production, as pets, or meat producers, it is important to take care of them and be ready for any such situation. If you are new to goats, then you won't know how to look for those signs, and if you do see it, you won't automatically realize it. So, here are some ways to find out whether your goat is showing signs of unhealthiness because the sooner you spot it and treat them, the better.

Stressful Goats

When you get a new goat, they might get stressed because of the change in their surroundings. You will find your goat eating less or nothing at all. They might not drink water, or come out to play with the rest of the herd. If you see one of these signs, then it's time to act.

Posture of Your Goat

Healthy goats have erect postures. You will not find any drooping ears or shoulders. You will notice that they hold their heads and tails up. The eyes of healthy goats are shiny, glossy, and sharp. So if you notice any contrary signs in your goat, take them to the veterinarian, and have them checked. Furthermore, if you see your goat in an awkward posture, such as trying to relieve themselves awkwardly, or stretching more than they should, then it is also a sign of some illness.

Slow Movements

When you see that your goat is not their usual self or not active the way they usually are, there may be something wrong, and you will need to have it fixed immediately.

Strange Ways of Bleating

Goats usually bleat ceaselessly when they are lonely or scared or hungry. They also cry unusually when they are not comfortable, either because they have some digestive issues, or they have an injury. The time of birth is also noisy at times because of the pain of delivery. Look out for these cries, and take action if you find anything out of the ordinary.

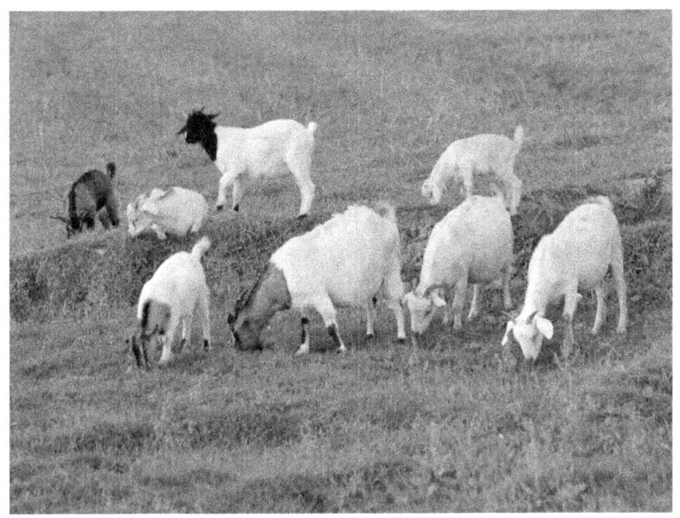

Temperature of their Body

A goat's normal body temperature ranges around 101 – 104 Fahrenheit. If you observe an unusual increase or decrease in their temperature, then it is a sign they are not doing well.

Trembling of Your Goat

Shivering in the cold or shivering in any way is not normal. Put them under blankets, and in their warm shelter, and if they continue shivering, take them to the vet.

Bloating

When you observe their midsection is swelling, this is a sign of bloating. Again, it should be treated by a vet.

.

Not Mixing with the Herd

Goats are social herd animals. If you see they have suddenly changed their habits, if they prefer isolation, aren't taking a normal amount of food and water, and keep lying around for an unusual length of time, then there is something wrong with them.

Limping

If you see your goat limping, there must be something wrong with their legs or feet, and a vet should be consulted. .

There are some other signs. If there's something wrong with their coat, and you see it is getting dull. Also, if they not urinating properly, or the color of their urine has changed. Or, if they are passing loose or strange feces. Pale gums may also well be a sign of sickness. A runny nose, coughing, strange breathing with weird noises, dull eyelids, blisters in their mouth or around the nose, are all indications you should take them to a vet.

Common Health Problems

When you have bought yourself a good quality goat for a pet, or for milk breeding or as meat producer, you must do thorough research about their needs, environment, and what are some of the common health problems. Sometimes, knowing some basics about them prevents the condition from worsening. Before buying a goat, do check out the animals around that goat, and the facilities of the farm. Goat vaccinations are very important so don't be lazy in regards to them. Moreover, if any disease is contagious you will need to separate that goat from the rest of the herd to avoid it from spreading.

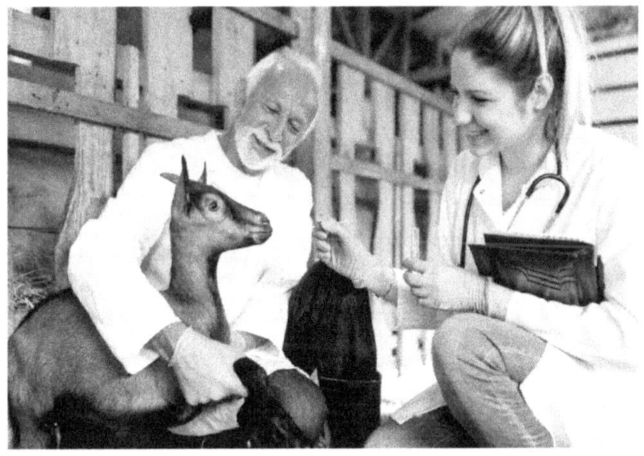

Here are some of the most common diseases/health problems in goats, and they will help you to understand things better.

Overeating – Clostridium Perfringens, Type C and D

This is called the overeating disease. It comes suddenly. The fastest, the healthiest and fittest animal, who will be fine one day, might be found dead the next day. You may think you never saw any symptoms. This usually happens with young goats when you wean them and put them on feed. They start eating abundantly, and contract Clostridium Perfringens infection. Sudden death occurs. There is no treatment as such because you will not get any time, so you must guard your goat against this infection.

Tetanus – Clostridium Tetani

Whenever we have a puncture wound from a rusty nail, we take a tetanus injection. The same is the case with goats. If and when they have any broken skin and wounds, they may have Clostridium Tetani. This organism is found very commonly in soil, so you will need tetanus injections to treat it. Signs of tetanus are joint stiffness, muscle pain, and you will notice them walking like they are on their toes in a hump. After a little time, their stance will lock up, and paralysis will attack their diaphragm. They won't be able to breathe and will die. Vaccinations are the best chance to prevent it.

Sore Mouth/Orf

This is a viral infection. Sores and pustules form in the goat's nose and mouth. It is like chicken pox in children. You will see a little scab right in the corner of the mouth. It heals by itself, just like chickenpox, if it is on a mild level. These animals have a high level of immunity so they will hardly get it again. But it becomes a problem if an adult goat catches it on their teats, and the young ones go to nurse, and she doesn't let them. Equally, if baby goats get them on their mouth, it makes it difficult for them to nurse. In either case, the young goat will starve. Therefore, isolate the sick goat, and clean them properly. There is a vaccine against it.

Urinary Calculi

In this disease, stones are found in the goat's urethra. It is common in both males and females, but it troubles males the most. These stones are usually the result of imbalance in the diet. Ask your local vet for all the information when you find or notice this in your goat.

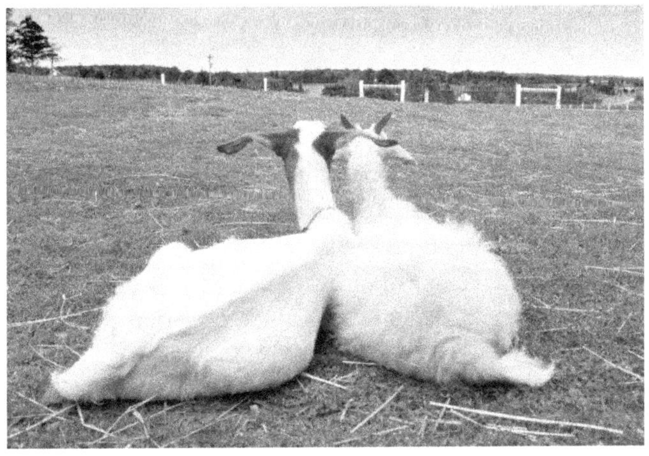

Pregnancy Toxemia

This is common in fat goats. Those who don't get much exercise typically get this. The other reason goats get this is when they are two to three months away from kidding. Suddenly there is a lot of rain, their blood glucose level drops, and they are vulnerable to this illness. Oral electrolytes do the job here, and if you drench them in hot water and Propalene glycol, in about fifteen minutes they will start walking again.

Coccidiosis

It is very common in goats. It doesn't mean they will show any clinical signs or are suffering from any disease. It is a parasite, and it is present in all the herds. It takes advantage when the animal becomes stressed. It will multiply. Medications are available for treatment and prevention.

Caseous Lymphadenitis (CL)

It is caused by Corynebacterium. You will see a golf-ball sized lump around the throat or in front of the shoulder. It can be treated and removed. Flush it with Iodine, and keep the animal isolated for some time. It doesn't affect that animal's meat if they are a meat producer. The real problem is when they keep recurring in other places. Vaccine only helps to control it, and there is no permanent cure. Also this organism is contagious. Contact your vet and ask for their guidance.

Contagious Foot Rot

This is caused by Fusobacterium necrophorum. It is common where there are lots of greenery and mud due to a lot of rain. If one goat gets this, the whole herd will get it. You can treat the foot with copper Sulphate, and all the herd around that animal. Antibiotics are used to treat this foot rot. Immunity against it is not possible. Ask your vet for other suggestions against it.

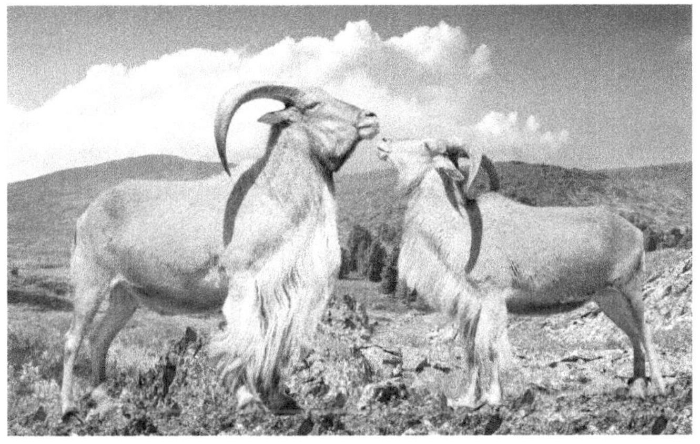

White Muscle Disease (Vitamin E/Selenium Deficiency)

There are some parts of the world where the soil is deficient in Selenium, and so the hay is also deficient in Selenium. You vet will tell you if there are any areas around your town. Supplements are given to goats over two to three days to make up the inadequacy. You will normally see this in baby goats. They will be fine from all angles, only they won't be able to stand on their feet.

These are the most common health problems found in goats, but it is always recommended to contact your local veterinarian and they will guide you further with your situation.

Chapter Summary

- Health and wellbeing of goats are very important to keep them healthy, active. This is for your benefit too.
- Goat grooming requires meticulous and careful steps; this includes bathing, brushing, clipping, and trimming their hooves.
- The first step is to brush their coat. You will need a soft brush and a curry comb. Start by gliding the curry comb in circular movements from neck to legs to abdomen and all the way to their legs. Then use a soft brush in the same way.
- Goats need bathing periodically. You can start by wetting them down, applying liquid shampoo or soap, carefully avoiding their eyes, and then rinsing them.

- Clipping or shearing your goat in summer would help them keep warm and free from bugs, flies and fleas. Make sure you do it carefully without hurting them.

- Trimming your goat's hooves are also necessary. But it is recommended to ask any expert to do it because there is a blood vessel in their foot, and, if you're not careful, you can hurt your goat badly.

- Daily exercises for goats are necessary to keep them fit and active. You can use a dog to run after them, you can run with them, and when you stop, they will stop. .

- Keep a close eye on your goats to observe any signs of unhealthiness.

- If you notice your goat is behaving a little oddly, or is stressed, you must check why they are behaving so.

- When you see your goat limping, it is also one of the signs that something is not right with their legs or feet.

- Goats are very active animals, so when you notice that your goat is not moving much, or is acting very lazily, then it is a sign that something is wrong.

- When your goat cries or screams without any apparent reason and doesn't stop, then you will need to check out what is wrong with them.

- When you see your goat shivering, or you observe their body temperature is too high, or lower than normal, it's a sign that something is going on and you need to see what it is.

- Bloating in goats is very abnormal so when you notice anything like it, take immediate measures.

- Goats are herd animals, so it is unlike them to prefer isolation. This is often a sign they are not feeling good.

- There are some common health problems found in goats too. Contagious foot rot is caused by Fusobacterium necrophorum, in which their hoof starts to rot because of wet mud where this bacteria lives.

- Sores at the corner of goats mouths are very common.

- Overeating is also common, caused by Clostridium Tetani. The animal will seem well, and will die suddenly.

- Urinary calculi, Pregnancy Toxemia, Coccidiosis, White Muscle Disease, Pink eye, Caseous Lymphadenitis (CL) and Tetanus are also very common diseases found in goats.

In the next chapter you will learn….

CHAPTER FIVE

BREEDING TIME

Goats have a specific breeding time which starts when they reach puberty. There comes a time when female goats heat up, and mate with male goats and that results in the impregnation of the females. However, goats have a particular time when this process can take place. Male goats are called bucks, whereas female goats are called does. If you want your goats to have babies then you will need to know all the things about the breeding time. What specific time it comes around, when you should put your does and bucks together, for how much time, at what age your goats are able to mate or reach puberty, and every other thing. The more you know, the easier it is to gain the possible advantage.

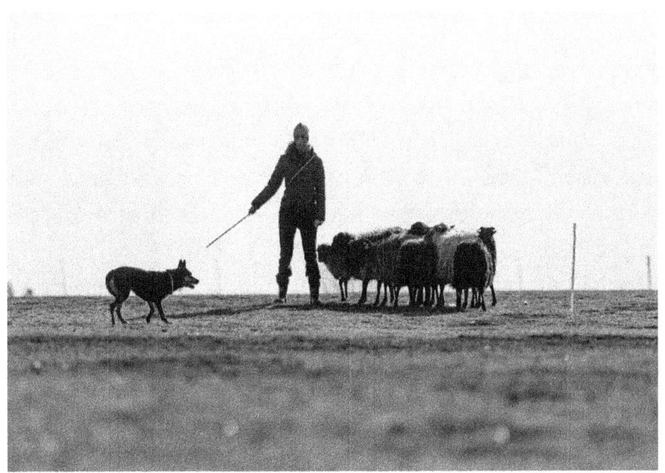

Specific Breeding Time in Goats

The preferred breeding time for goats is around late summer or fall, because this will ensure the kidding season to be warmer, which would be around 4 to 5 months of the pregnancy. Meat goats usually breed the whole year around, whereas dairy goats breed around fall, starting from August to November or December. Breeders usually choose this time because they don't want kids coming all year. Most of the does have the estrous cycle around every 18 to 21 days, which is also called the heat cycle. The estrous cycle is the time from one cycle to the next.

How to Know Your Doe is Ready for Breeding?

Does usually reach the age of puberty from 4 to 12 months. Nutrition, breed type, environmental conditions, and their state of health also play a major part. Bucks reach their puberty from 4 months and can start breeding, but it is advisable to wait for them to be a year old. How do you know your doe is ready to breed? How would you tell they are heating up? If your bucks and does have only a fence between them, you will notice they would like to keep close to each other. Does will start hanging out near the bucks, and away from the herd. They will discharge a substance from their vulva which will also become swollen, they will wag their tails a lot, and they will also start shouting quite a bit.

The bucks also show clear signs when the breeding time arrives. They will start to stink a lot. You will notice urination on their beards, and they start making some funny blabbering noises with their upper lip curled up.

Mating Time

A year-old buck can breed up to 10 does at one time, a 2-year-old can impregnate up to 25 goats and a 3-year-old can breed up to 40 does simultaneously. When the buck is ready to mate, this time is known as rut because they become obsessed with females. A doe is ready for breeding when they get around 70 to 85 pounds in weight. As much as their age matters, the weight matters more; it is important to make sure the doe is physically ready to be bred and can carry a baby. Does heat up for around 12 to 36 hours, and this is called their reproductive cycle. During this period, they get receptive and let the buck breed them. They don't usually get pregnant the first time, but eventually they do if the buck is kept with them.

Gestation Period in Goats

When the breeding is done, your doe will conceive and the gestation period begins. This period in goats generally stretches around 148 to 152 days, which is around 5 to 5 and a half months. Pregnant goats require great care; pregnancy takes a toll on the mother so full care, with meticulously given food, is imperative. How will you know your doe has conceived? A sonogram would do the job; otherwise it is difficult to tell until late pregnancy. You will notice that your doe has stopped bleating needlessly, is not wagging their tail that much, and is not as interested in the buck as she was before. So, after making sure your doe is pregnant, you will need to give them a light diet for the first two months. Dry hay or grains or whatever your goat loves. Make sure their diet is light, and after two months you will need to increase their diet a bit. Add in more grains for nutrition. Also, consult your vet. For the last 15 to 20 days, when your doe gets very big, you will need to watch them carefully because they get uncomfortable and stop eating. You will need to make sure their shelter is comfortable for them, and they are eating properly because they will need strength at the time of kidding.

You can also give them protein supplements or other things for nutrition, and let them sit wherever they want to because they will get stressed, and it will affect their health. During the last days, you must keep them in yards where they are comfortable, and the kidding time will be easier for them.

Kidding Time

After the completion of usually 140 days, your doe can be due any time. Does are known to give birth to 2 to 3 litters at a time. You will need to be extra prepared when that time comes. You will need to be there for your doe when they go into labor because it will be good for your bond. This process is awe-inspiring because seeing the miracle of life is simultaneously a beautiful and anxious time.

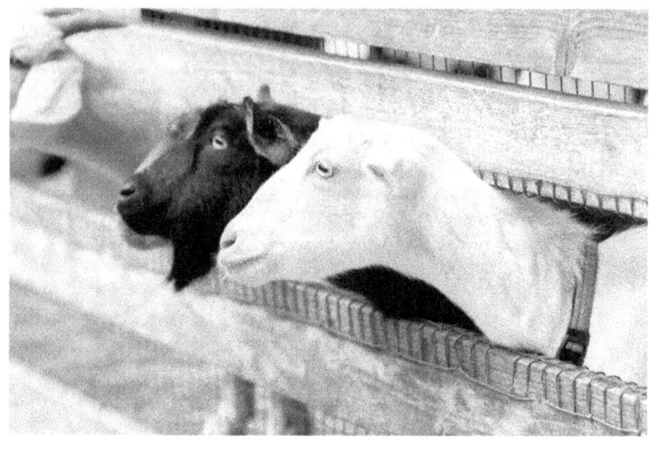

How would you know the doe is in labor? The labor consists of three stages. The first stage is to notice the signs of labor in your doe. You will see your doe's udder swelling, either 2 to 4 weeks before kidding, or right before kidding. They will get hard because they fill them up. You will also notice the baby inside, or the mother has drooped and she will have a sunken side and prominent hip bones. This sign is usually visible during the last 4 to 5 days. The doe's tail ligaments will begin to loosen, and when you are actually able to hold the tail head completely, then your doe will go into labor in about 24 hours. Another sign is that your doe's vulva will loosen. Discharge of vaginal fluid is also a sign. Your doe will separate herself from the herd when the time arrives, usually within 24 hours. They also paw the ground, and look for the right spot to give birth. You might see your doe yawning right before labor. The last sign you will see are the contractions. Their tails arch up and down along with their back.

The second stage is known as active labor. The baby will push out. At first, you will see a bag and then it will break, and then a pair of feet if the baby is in normal position. The feet will face the ground. If all is well, your doe will be able to push the babies out with no problem at all. If you see your doe pushing with no result for an hour or more, then it is time to go and ease the process for her. Sometimes babies get stuck in the canal, or with each other, or simply can't come out, so some emergency plan will save you last minute trouble. Contact your vet beforehand to ask for assistance at the time of need. After giving birth, you will need to make sure your doe starts nuzzling and licking their babies to make a bond with them. They usually do that by themselves.

The third stage is called removing the placenta. This is very important. The goat will expel the remaining placenta in about a day, and if any of it remains inside, it will be the cause of infection. Some does will take time to remove the entire placenta, but if it takes too much time then contact your vet. Do not pull it out of the doe's body. If your doe eats her own placenta, then that is normal and good for their health. Bouncing your doe's belly will make sure all the placenta comes out of it.

Some Useful Tips for Breeding Season

When you purchase your goats, invest in the good quality of your buck. Because they will be 50% of the herd's genetics, so you will want a healthy and fit buck to pass this on to the kids. The extra expense will benefit you in the long run. Farmers or breeders usually keep does and bucks separated, so you will need secure fencing to keep the buck reaching the does in the breeding season. Because the buck will be healthy, and they will test the strength of the fence, strong fencing is recommended. When you keep your buck separated, make sure you keep another male with them because they are herd animals, and will get lonely.

Once your buck has finished breeding all the does, you can keep them with the herd until the kidding season. Separate your buck after that because you don't want them to be nosy once your does kidding season begins. Some does will recycle again after that, but if you don't want them to breed again, keep them separated. You can keep a track of all the kids. If your does start breeding around September, then the kids would come around the end of January or the start of February.

A little cold weather for kidding is good because worms, flies and other parasites won't be there to trouble the baby goats. When they are born in winter, they learn to cope with the weather, and to be fit and healthy in that season. Breeding throughout the year is not recommended as it will put the life of your does at greater risk and jeopardize their health.

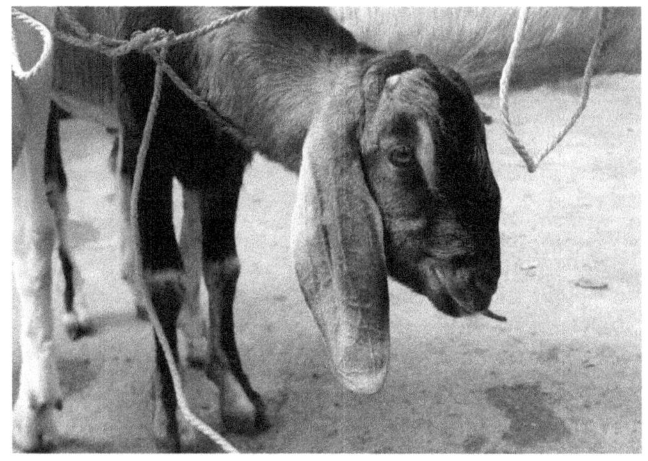

Caring for New-Born Goats

Baby goats are fun and entertaining to be around. They will do funny things and keep you amused by playing tricks, jumping, and their cute little habits. It is imperative to know how to care for them even before they arrive. The handler or the breeder must know how to do it better than their mother to ensure healthy growth. Some things you must do in advance is to know how to make the fencing secure for them, how to feed the kids and the mother, and how to make the environment safe for them.

Taking care of newborn babies will make sure no death occurs, and they grow to be healthy and fit, and be amazing at milking. Taking care of them from the start will save you a lot of future problems, and make your job hassle-free.

Goats eat greens, fresh hay, and grains, so a combination of all these things, along with fresh water, would give them nutrition to nurse their new-born babies. These are the main source of their nutrition, and will keep them healthy. .

Immediate Care for New-Born Babies

Most importantly, check it they are breathing and alive. Remove the sticky layer covering them, especially from their mouth and nose so they can breathe properly. If they are weak, then insert a little straw to help them in breathing. Keep them warm. When the weather is warm, their mother will do the job by licking them and placing them near her, but if the weather is cold, then you will need to take them inside. Bring the mother and the kids to an enclosed, sheltered, and warm space. You can spread a thick bedding of dry hay to make the kids comfortable. You can also use a heating lamp, but make sure you don't let them get too near it. The kids will have an umbilical cord attached to them, cut it to 1.5 inches, using a pair of sterile scissors, then dip into iodine solution to make sure no infection could get inside of it. The babies will find their way around, nursing onto mother's udders. Help them to suck if they can't find their way.

What to Feed Your Baby Goats?

When you give the doe all the proper nutrition she needs, she will be able to nurse all her babies at the same time. But if the mother is not able to fulfil the need, then you will need to bottle feed the babies. Cow milk is not suitable for baby goats. You will need milk with colostrum which will give the same nutrients as their mother's milk. But it is important to know how to bottle feed them. You will need to make them learn how to use those bottles. They will not want to take it, but you will need to push gently, by opening their mouths and squirting milk in. You might need to enlist the help of a friend in gently opening the baby's mouth. If the young goat resists, then stay patient, and keep making repeated attempts throughout the day. If the problem persists then it's a good idea to take the kid to a vet; the health of a new-born goat is delicate and they may be in danger of dehydration if they keep refusing the bottle. Generally, you will discover that goats who are bottle fed will become more closely bonded to humans. Assuming you are successful, the kids will need feeding three to four times in a single day for the first four weeks, and then you can reduce it. When they get above 6 weeks, they will need to be transferred to other feed simultaneously, and they may have a hard time of it. They will experience issues in digestion if the balance between the two isn't kept. They might start bloating, so make sure they do not switch to hay or grass too fast, and they don't over-eat. Because they are used to their mama's milk, their bellies will give them a tough time at the beginning.

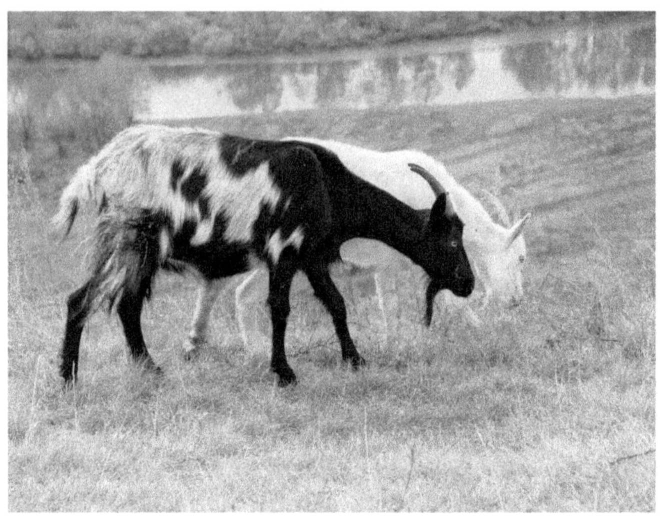

When a baby goat is not taken care of properly, they will die. Also don't give goat treats to babies because goats eat hay, grass and grains. Treats are not healthy for the babies. You must place them separately from the other goats when they are very small, and keep them with their mother, but don't try to keep them pinned at one place. Free them occasionally to mix with the rest of the herd.

Some other tips for breeding are that you must decide beforehand when you want your does to breed, and which time of the year you want to kid. You will need to prepare your does for this process before the time comes. In this process, you should give some concentrates to your does two weeks prior to breeding. Another thing to remember is that after breeding is done, you will need to design a quality nutritional regime for your does, so they will be able to conceive and deliver strong and healthy babies.

Training Baby Goats

When you have many baby goats it is hard to feed them without them jumping onto you, and nibbling you everywhere. It is imperative to train them early so they don't grow up to be rude and misbehaving adults. While feeding, when they start to jump on you, gently put them down. Keep repeating this because they will need to know it is not nice behaviour. Don't give them your fingers to suck because if you do, they will keep doing it. Bear in mind they have sharp teeth at the back of their mouths, and they can hurt you. It is much better to not let them do this from the start. When they head push you, don't let them do this. Gently stop them every single time. It might seem cute behavior when they are small, but when they grow, it gets dangerous. It is better to get them out of the habit at an early age.

Another way to train baby goats is to show love to them. You will need to spend a lot of time with them. You will need to give your time to them to create this bond. Because of this they will know not to fear you. Whenever you get near them, they will need to know they are going to be safe; it's a good investment for the future if you create that bond. That way they won't constantly be in your face. You will have caressed them enough so that they won't need to do that.

Another thing you can do is to give them space where they can have their fun. They are still nursing, so you don't want them to do anything too complicated; just give them some things to jump onto and they will do great. Moreover, don't try to chase baby goats, and pick them up when they're in mid-stride. You must tell this to your whole family, and whoever is involved with you in training and looking after them. They feel insecure when they're picked up this way. When you do this, baby goats will start running away from you, and you don't want them to do that, so avoid the practice. In short, give them lots of love, keep them where they like to be, and don't pick them up mid-stride. This way, while growing up, they will be doing all sorts of stuff which you want them to do, and going places where you want them to. So, you see, it is not some extraordinary rocket science. Stick to simple and basic techniques, and you and your baby goats will be doing just fine.

Some other tips are that in order to avoid certain diseases, or fleas, bugs and other parasites, keep the space you are using clean and dry, and do not let any parasites breed. Moreover, keep that place well ventilated, and well lit, so that whatever insects or parasites are crawling in there, will die and don't create problems for those newborns. Keep the fence secured to ensure that no predator could attack those babies. If you have high-extension wire and fencing, then be extra watchful to not let those kids wander near them, or they will get zapped and could die. In addition, if you have placed some things for their jumping, make sure they are not high, or they will fall and hurt themselves. Good health and a safe environment are very important for their hassle-free growth and survival.

Chapter Summary

- Goats have a certain breeding time which starts from fall, and continues until late winter, from August till December or January.

- Meat producing goats breed throughout the year.

- A female goat is called a doe. They are ready for breeding when they get a year old, or around 70 to 85 pounds in weight. Weight is necessary for them to carry a baby or they will die.

- When a doe is in heat, you will notice them wagging their tails ceaselessly. They will bleat like crazy, and they will like to be around bucks more than usual.

- This heat cycle is also called an estrous cycle, and this continues for around 12 to 26 hours during this breeding season.

- The male goat is called a buck. They are to breed when they get a year-old, and can breed around 10 does at a time. A 2-year-old can breed upto 25, and a 3-year-old can breed up to 40 does simultaneously.

- When a buck is ready, you will notice them sniffing, blabbering, and urinating all over themselves.

- Don't breed your goats all year; this will weaken them, as pregnancy takes a toll on the mother's body.

- When a doe is receptive, she stands and let a buck breed her. It is not necessary that they conceive on the first attempt.

- Gestation period revolves around 145 to 152 days in goats. During this period, and especially in the last two months, does require extra care and attention.

- They need extra food which would provide them nutrition, and will help them in labor.

- When a doe is in labor, you will see their udders swelling and they will get hard, the baby inside the mother will give a drooping shape to the belly, their tail ligaments will start to get loose, and there will be a discharge of vaginal fluid.

- During active labor, the doe will push out the babies. The bag will come out and it will break. If the situation gets serious, you will need to be prepared, or call your vet.

- The doe will expel placenta on her own. Don't pull it out of her body. If it doesn't come out in 2 days, you need to call a vet.

- Does eating their placenta is very normal; in fact it gives them strength.

- Newborn babies require immediate care. It is important the mother licks them clean, and keep them warm to build their bond.

- If the weather is not warm, then you will need to bring them somewhere sheltered. You can also use a heater, but don't let the kids get near it.

- If the umbilical cord is longer than 1.5 inches then you will need to cut it with a pair of sterile scissors, and dip them in iodine solution to avoid any infections.

- Babies usually find a way around their mother's udders, but if they won't, you will need to help them.

- If the mother is not letting the baby nurse, then you will need to bottle feed them.

In the next chapter you will learn….

CHAPTER SIX

COMMON MISTAKES TO AVOID

We have talked about how to purchase a goat? How to purchase a good quality goat? How to know where you will find good goats? What to see when you go to buy a goat? What things you must know beforehand when you want to buy a baby goat? How to feed your goat? What to feed your goat? How to handle your goat? How to train your goat? How to give them a good and warm shelter? How to handle a pregnant goat? How to look after them when it comes to cleaning, bathing and clipping? How to observe signs of unhealthiness? How to deal with your goat when they get sick? What to do when you see something is wrong with them? What is the best time for breeding? How to breed them? How to handle the kidding process? How to look after newborns? We have talked about all these things in detail, but people still make some common mistakes, thinking they won't do any harm. Unfortunately, such mistakes can end up with the owner having the sad experience of an animal's death. In this chapter, we will talk about what those common mistakes are, how you can avoid them, and how you can make this journey the greatest, not the worst, time.

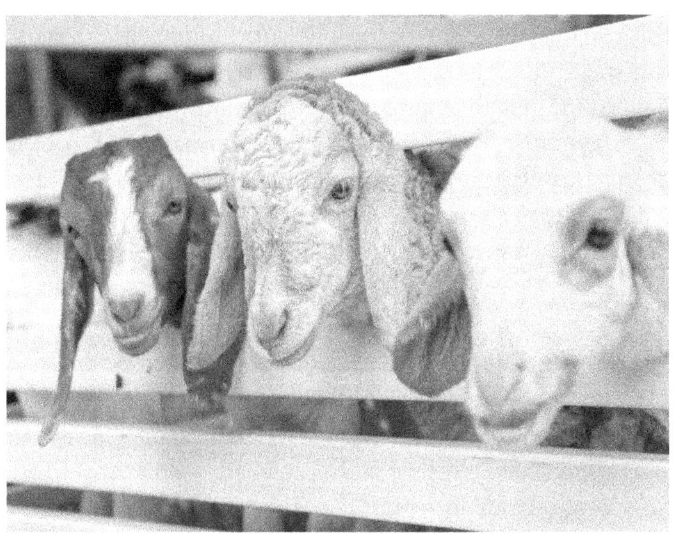

Things Not to Do When You Buy a Goat

Goats are herd animals, and they don't like it when they are lonely. Always purchase two goats at first. This is important, and new goat owners often think they can overlook this simple rule. Let's imagine that you think this will not cause a problem for you, and you have a pregnant doe that is due in a month. You have made a special goat fence, which is different than that used for other cattle, you have put the goat there, secured it tightly, and the next day you come to discover there is no goat to be seen! She has run away, and you will have to take a lot of trouble in finding her. You might get her back, or you might not. Maybe you'll find her somewhere with other goats, and the people around would tell you she came here, and never moved when she saw the other goats who could be her companions. What is the lesson here? That you shouldn't ever make this error again; it might look like nothing big at the start, but the end result can cost you dearly. Another point to bear in mind is that, since they are friendly animals, goats can benefit from having the company of other domesticated animals. Dogs, cats, horses, cows or sheep - if you have these on your homestead, your goats will be happier and more content from interacting with them.

Things to Avoid When You Are Setting a Homestead

When you set up a homestead, there are some factors you can't control, but many times there are things which are your own doing, and those decisions make your homesteading life harder than it already is. We will discuss those things, so you can avoid these pitfalls.

Never purchase a goat on an impulse. Impulse buying might seem like fun on the day, but later on, it isn't. Just because a goat looks cute and healthy doesn't mean there won't be any other issues with them. Don't buy a goat online, or from Craigslist, merely on an impulse because the consequences might well be dire. Do all the research, and ask all the important questions; you will find that initial hard work will pay off in a great way for you. Another thing you may well have heard is that if you raise your animals naturally, you will not face any problems. This is a myth. Raising your animals naturally won't protect them against any sickness, worms, diseases, and all the other hazards. You really do need artificial help alongside natural methods. Don't be reluctant to use modern methods where they are useful.

Nowadays, whenever we want to start something new, we read blogs and watch vlogs on the internet, and we may fall into the trap of believing everything we see that's popular on Google. This really is a big mistake. For example, you will read that when you feed your goats properly, they will not eat any poisonous plants. This is completely wrong, and you should rid your mind of any such complacent notions. When you free your goats on pasture, or your garden, you must make sure there are no poisonous plants like Rhododendron, Laurel Mountains, or Azaleas. Your animals will immediately go to these and will start eating them. If you see such plants, make certain you have them removed. The best thing to do is to ask for any local person's advice, anyone who has tons of experience in these matters; they would be able to guide you properly. The second thing you can do is go for printed information such as books or magazines. The last thing to do is to depend on blogs and other internet stuff. This is not to say they don't sometimes have the right information, but the internet can also be an untrustworthy place, and such sites can be misleading. If you read or see any vlogs, make sure they have been in existence for a long time, that you can rely on the expertise of those on it, and that these people have a lot of experience in their subject. You are risking your capital and a good deal of time and emotional investment, as well as the lives and health of your animals, so go to the most reputable places when you're looking for information.

It's sensible to start small. Don't go and buy a lot of goats, or it will become a frustration, and you will end up doing no work at all. There will be no fun or enjoyment for you in this. You don't want the whole endeavour to become a chore, or something that causes you undue anxiety. Planning in advance is also necessary. Get your infrastructure ready before getting a goat, and you will have an easier time.

Things You Should Avoid When You Have Goats

Make sure, whatever place you are keeping goats on your property, that place should be good for them. When we see a green land with thick lush grass, we automatically think this will be the perfect place for our goats. When we see a dry land with dried grass or mature wood, with no grass at all, we think this place won't be a good home for our goats. That is because we are observing the two landscapes with a wholly different set of values from what is the practical requirements for goats. The actual truth is quite the opposite. Don't be misled by what seems an idyllic environment. Most of the worm problems your goats have to endure in their lives are caused and worsened when they spend most of their time in green pastures with wet land. That's where all those worms and parasites multiply, and get on the coats and skins of your herd. So, this is one thing you must avoid. If your goats are going there continuously, it won't improve their condition; it will only worsen it. This doesn't mean it's impossible to keep goats on pasture, but you are going to multiply the risks of parasite infestation. Prevention is better than cure, and the best thing you can do about worms is to decrease the chances of your animals catching them in the first place.

The second thing to remember is that you make sure where you are getting your goats from. It is not necessarily about the quality of the goats, or to check the facilities. It is about making sure you get the goats from the environment which you yourself have for them on your homestead or farm. A goat from a dry land with gravel, dry grass and hay, wouldn't do well in an environment with green grass, thick bushes, and damp land. That's because their living conditions are different, and animals usually don't thrive if you change the way they live. This is pretty simple; you can't make an animal that is from a colder area live in a hotter part of the world, and vice versa.

The third thing you must do, and not take it any less seriously than it already is, is to figure out how to deworm. Parasites and worms are common when it comes to goats and sheep. They are not usually common with other animals, but they will and do attack smaller animals such as goats and sheep, and drain the life out of them. Experts and farmers can discuss which deworming medicine to get and which not to, but the main thing is to monitor if that medicine is making progress or not. Do fecal egg count tests at least two or three times a week. If, after a week, you don't see the shine returning into your goat's eyes, then it will be time to change the medication. The medicines that have worked previously might not work this time because the worms are showing resistance; therefore fecal tests are important. You can certainly do fecal tests at home with a microscope. That's because it will be expensive to ship those feces, and also pay the lab's charges. So why not save your time and money by investing in a microscope, and checking it yourself? This gives you much greater control and awareness of the situation. This monitoring will tell you how your goat is doing. You might think you were providing the correct medications, then, quite unexpectedly, your goat dies. You will be shocked at what has happened. Fecal tests provide you with an unambiguous assessment of what is going on inside the bodies of your herd, whether they have worm infestations, and whether the parasites are increasing or declining.

The fourth thing to know is the mistake new owners tend to make by not placing a livestock guardian. If you have a small or a large area where your goats roam around, but you don't have a tight and secure fencing, you will certainly need a livestock guardian. It is up to you whichever animal you think would do the job, but you really will need one. Predators can come hunting for your goats, and it would be tragic to feed your animals to them. Also, baby goats are really small and vulnerable, and it is very easy for bobcats or foxes to take them away in the blink of an eye.

Another thing new owners must do, if you want to make a good herd, is to get a good quality doe. Don't simply go and buy the prettiest goat you like; as with many things in life, it is not about just looks. You will need to have a goat that is internal worm resistant, whose breed is known to be good mothers, and all the other elements. This will help you in developing a great herd. This is one of the most frequent mistakes made by new goat owners. Keep a good track of how they are doing.

Keep records: when you got them, when you bred them, when they kidded, how many were born, how many survived, how they are milking, everything should be written down. Because once they become two or three animals, you will start forgetting how they did, or how many kids a certain doe has. Good record keeping is a must for efficiency and professionalism.

Things to Avoid While Feeding Goats

When you are feeding your goats, and you are getting bales of dry hay, you will have noticed that it's covered in a sort of net to keep it from scattering. Handlers usually don't pay much attention to it, but this net can be very dangerous. Your goats legs or necks can get stuck, and it can cut through the skin. It is especially dangerous for baby goats because they will jump right in, will get their necks or legs caught, and won't be able to untangle themselves. You will need to remove it before placing it in the barn for their feeding. Use a small knife, cut right through it, and remove its threads, and then the hay is good to go in the barn. To avoid waste, you can use huge barn trays with metal iron bars, otherwise known as feeders; these are where you can place all the dry hay in the center of the feeder, and your goats can eat through the bars without wasting a lot. You cannot stop waste altogether, but this will keep it to a reasonable minimum. Another advantage of feeders is that they keep the hay clean; if you simply put the hay on the ground and allow the goats to access it, they will inevitably dirty it underfoot, and urinate on it. Goats can be picky eaters, and they will be disinclined to eat dirty hay. Ignoring factors like this increases wastage and adds to your expenses.

When you start overfeeding your goat, or they start eating too much wet stuff and grains, they have a tendency to bloat. In bloating their body starts to swell and the gas builds up; if not treated at the time, it could result in the death of the animal. Goats love grains, so it is for the goat owner to not overfeed them. You will see a lot of packaged goat treats on the market, and you will want to indulge your goats. That's also one of the most common errors made by new goat owners. They start giving these treats, and their proper food, dry hay and grass, gets put on the sideline. As a result, the goats get sick, and if not taken care of, they will die. Remember that dry hay and grains are their natural diet, so stick to them.

Things to Avoid During Breeding Season

The first and foremost thing is to make sure your doe is 1-year-old and is about 70 to 85 pounds in weight to be bred so that she can carry the baby. The weight is the most important thing in this matter. Also, breeding your goats throughout the year is not good for their health. Pregnancy takes its toll on the mother, and breeding them again and again would result in the exhaustion and possible death of the doe. Even the babies they produce won't be healthy. Breeding once a year is the recommended way to go. Don't try to breed a buck and a doe that are not equal in terms of size and weight. They may harm each other if one is bigger in size. During the time of kidding, things can quickly go wrong. You will need a plan beforehand. Delivering babies is a difficult process, and your goat can have problems. You will need to decide then and there what to do, otherwise your goat's life is at stake. In case of these scenarios, you will need a fully written-out plan, so that you can help your animal, and not feel guilty afterwards because you couldn't do anything for them at the time. New-born babies can get sick, so you will need supplies to hand to enable you to help them. Make sure you have the important and general medications in your home.

Some Other Common Mistakes an Owner Must Avoid

When you have goats, you must keep some things to avoid trouble and hassle at the last minute. Because you will need them, and the trips to get those things, or journeys to vets, would take a lot of time when you actually need them immediately. Some people don't keep emergency stuff, and that's one of the most common and deadliest mistakes they make. Some general medications should always be to hand when you have goats. Read the labels in advance to make sure you are familiar with the directions, and know how to use them. Keep them at your farm or homestead. Goats usually have internal parasite issues. They will almost inevitably get it at some time or the other, so the time it will take you to take them to a vet would worsen the situation. That is why you will need some wormers to keep the condition from getting very bad. You must rotate between them. Check where the goats are getting the worms from because, although medication is good, you may have to take steps to deal with the outside environment. New breeders don't know how to deal with emergency situations like these, or, to take another example, when your goat suddenly starts limping or catches influenza or a fever. Doing some research beforehand, and getting some guidance from a local vet, would help to cope with these difficulties. You will be able to deal with these issues, and stop them from getting worse. Breeders cannot take their goats to a vet for every problem, or it would become impossible for them to afford goats. Therefore, learn things, try to deal with them by yourself at first, and then if that won't work, you can take them to a veterinarian.

Things to Avoid During Training Goats

While training goats, people usually forget that each animal is different than the other, even if is from the same mother. So, when you start to train them, no matter whether you train them individually, or together as a herd, each and every goat will take their own time to pick up what you want them to do. Their learning style and the time they take will be different. This won't make any goat less than who they are, but the owner will have to remember this. They have their own personalities. This requires patience and repetition. Yelling at them, or hitting them, won't quicken this process. On the contrary, they will get stressed and most likely refuse to cooperate. You can actually make your goats learn all sorts of stuff. You can walk with them, run with them, but all you have to do show tolerance and self-restraint. You will need to show your goat each and everything, step by step, and maybe give them treats when they perform well. But don't force them into things. Don't push or pull them. They are very intelligent animals, and they will eventually understand what you want of them. But they will very likely take their time to learn. Let them pick it up at their own pace, and they will come around to it.

In addition, make sure that whatever breeds you want to get, you do all the research beforehand so that you can avoid all the stress. People usually don't do their homework, and end up having bad experiences. Preparation, as is the case with so many things, is the key; a little bit of time and thought in advance can save you and your animals a great deal of trouble later on.

Another point; don't leave the ground wet where you leave your goats for pasturing, or where they roam around, because it will result in foot rotting, and your goat will suffer because you didn't take notice of the sticky mud present in such areas.

Chapter Summary

- Don't ever buy a single goat because they are herd animals, and the chances of their running away are high. You might find them, or you might end up regretting your decision altogether.

- When you want to set up a homestead, you don't always have any control over natural elements, but you must make sure there are no poisonous trees in the vicinity.

- Never buy a goat on an impulse. Just because a goat is pretty, and seems fine, doesn't mean you buy it immediately. Do your research thoroughly.

- Look beyond Craigslist. If a goat is on sale, make sure you try to figure out why that goat is on sale and no others.

- Mountain Laurels, Azaleas and Rhododendrons are poisonous trees and your goats will die if they eat them. Make sure you remove them.

- There is misinformation on the internet that when you feed your goats they will not go to poisonous plants. This is completely wrong.

- Go and ask someone from your locality who is experienced in goats. They will be able to guide you properly and thoroughly.

- Start small. Don't go big very early, or things will no longer be fun and enjoyable for you.

- Wherever you plan to keep your goats, make sure that place is the same where you have bought your goat from. Changing their environment won't do the animal any good.

- Green grass, lush pasture, and wet ground are not good for goats. These are the places where parasites and worms grow.

- When your goats spend too much time in those lands, they get the problem of internal worms, and if not treated, they just die.

- When you do deworming, you must monitor it very closely. If, in a week, you see that medication is not doing its work, then change it.

- Get a microscope, and do those fecal tests yourself.

- If a medication worked the previous time, it doesn't mean it will work again. Worms build a resistance to it, so it is recommended to change it.

- Another mistake goat owners usually make is, they don't place a livestock guardian. When your animals wander around your land, wild animals and predators are prone to attack.

- Don't overfeed your goats. Don't indulge them, or it will create problems for them

- Don't give your goats those fancy goat treats you see in the market; they are not good.

- The breeding age of your doe is one year, and when she weighs around 70 to 85 pounds. Weight is necessary.

- Having an emergency plan at the time of birthing is necessary in case things go wrong.

- Don't pull the placenta from the mother. She will expel it herself.

- Keep some general medications at your farm or homestead so you don't have to run to your vet every single time.

- Do research about the breed you want to purchase beforehand.

In the next chapter you will learn….

CHAPTER SEVEN

CONCLUSION

People usually don't prefer goats as pets, even for their farm or homestead. They are not very common, because, in some respects, they are strange animals, and, at first, you may find them a little odd too. But when you decide to purchase one because you want to build a farm or homestead, then you will need to know some basics before going shopping. Firstly, you will have to decide on the breed. There are many breeds out there, but you will need to do thorough research about what kind would be feasible for you. In some states, goats in residential areas are illegal, so make sure you're not in this situation. Kikos are great if you want to buy male goats. Norwegian Dwarf goats are great for milk breeding, and Pygmy goats and Boer goats are good meat producers. Pygmy and Nigerian Dwarf goats are smaller and easy to look after. .

You will also need to know what age is best for adoption. When a baby goat is 2 weeks old, they are ideal to adopt because they will have nursed enough of their mother's milk, which is rich in Colostrum, and will have built up their immune system. You can also get 4 weeks old, or 6 weeks old, baby goats, for yourself, and adult goats too. Goats are herd animals and they are very social, so it is important to get two, even for a starter, otherwise they will get lonely, depressed, and possibly sick. Give your goats names, it will help you in training them.

Feeding a baby goat is a little tricky initially, but easy once you know how to do it. A 2 week old baby needs feeding 4 times a day. You will need to feed them the goat replacement milk with Colostrum. You will need a baby bottle and nipple.

Babies will need to be bottle trained because they won't know what it is. This will require patience, and a lot of time. When the baby gets to 4 weeks old, you will need to add dry hay and grains into their feed and gradually reduce their milk feeding. As for adult goats, 80% of their feed is dry hay, 15% grass and 5% grains. They don't need anything else in their food. Some nuts or vegetables as treats are also good. They love grains too, but the owner needs to give them a limited quantity because it is a cause of bloating.

Baby and adult goats both need a proper warm sheltered space with dry hay, clean bedding, and a draft free section. They are not the type of animal who can be allowed to stay outside all day and night. They are not weak animals, but they will suffer if exposed to extremes of temperature. Their soiled bedding must be changed for new and dry bedding every other day. Unused and leftover hay will come in handy here. A proper yard, where they can move freely and roam around, is also important. Include some things to climb onto because they love jumping. Sweep out this area every day. A normal 4-feet high fence is good for them, but if you have tall goats, then 5-feet is recommended.

Goats also need proper care and protection. When you purchase goats, you must also know they require proper and timely vaccinations against bacteria and parasites. They are usually disease resistant, but sometimes parasites reach them. The guidance of a veterinarian is recommended here. Their hooves also need trimming, but this should be done by an expert, otherwise your goat will suffer consequences. Bathing and brushing periodically is also imperative. Clipping or shaving twice a year should be done too.

There is a special fencing available for goats, which is not used for other animals. You can also do a temporary fencing which is usually done using Poly tape, a wire, or electric netting. This is used to keep stray animals and children from goats so that they won't disturb them. When your neighborhood isn't that safe, you can also use high wire fencing. It's not just wild animals who might want to prey on your goats; you could also run into the problem of human thieves as well, and this is a danger you will want to guard against in much the same way as you would protect the rest of your property. Permanent fencing is usually done to keep your goats from straying because they are inquisitive animals, and like to peek around everywhere. This kind of fencing will prevent them from wandering too far. It will also keep all the predators and hunters away. You can use wood panels, high-tensile wire, barbed or woven wire, and electric netting for perimeter fencing. A four-inch square fencing is ideal for goats, otherwise they will put their head through and hurt themselves.

Goats love jumping, so when you place water troughs, you will need to place a ramp inside it because babies will jump inside, and they will be able to climb back out safely. Alternatively, you can also go for smaller water troughs. When you use a bucket to feed them, make sure their handle is flat along with the rim because if it faces upward they will stick their head through, and babies can break their necks on it. Keep the fencing secured and locked at night. Baby goats must be secured safely away because they are the easiest of targets; they are less able to defend themselves or run away, and are therefore most susceptible to attack. Use high tensile fencing so that predators won't be able to come near it.

Handling your goat with care is essential. This will help you in the long-run and will keep your goat fit, healthy, and their productivity will be good. It will decrease their chances of catching illnesses. There are some basic traits to understand. Using those traits to your benefit, and managing your herd in accordance with them, will ease the entire process a great deal.

The most important thing to understand is that sheep and goats are not similar, and handling a sheep is completely different from handling a goat. Any kind of aggressive behavior by you will upset your goats, and they will not cooperate. Don't force your goats to do anything. This will frighten them. Goats also like to move in herds, and they have a flock queen who leads them, so the handler can encourage the queen to move forward, which, in turn, will move the entire flock. When they go to pasture, they tend to scatter away, so, to flock them together when there is a threat, don't push them to move. They may simply walk right back to where they were, or will refuse to walk at all. The handler can use a food bucket to lure them, or encourage the queen to.

Goats are intelligent animals and using their natural intelligence would provide their handler with an advantage. A trained livestock guard will also move them with ease. Ticking technique would also serve to a great extent. Their visual range is around 320 to 360 degrees, and they use this range to keep a track of their herd, and any incoming threat. Using their vision to move them, and incorporating food treats with it, will work considerably well for the handler. Handling them and making them do all these things will require patience. Animals can sense their handler's impatience, and will likely refuse to cooperate. Don't try to move large herds at the same time; it gets confusing for the animals.

Handling pregnant goats with caution and care is also necessary. The handler should keep an eye on their feed, especially during the later stages of pregnancy. If it is her first time, then you need to make her extra comfortable because they get jumpy. Newborns also require attention soon after their birth because they cannot look out for themselves, and are in danger of hypothermia. If the mother refuses to nurse them, then the handler must bottle feed them.

When your adult goat head butts you, or pushes you or jumps on you, then it is no longer cute and you need to work on that. You can flip them gently, stand over them, speak to them saying 'No', and tell them this behavior will not do. They will submit themselves in this position, and after that you allow them to stand upright. Make sure to caress them after that to show you still love them; this will help with your bond and they won't go away from you in either a physical or mental sense.

Training your goats helps with the release of stress because, when they are in the habit of doing things, the process will become easier, not only for them, but for the handler too. They learn quickly, but a lot of patience and repetitive measures are needed. Impatience or aggressive behavior has no place here. You can use special goat treats, and food, to lure them into doing things you want. If they are not behaving properly, use food because they are like most domesticated animals in that respect, they will probably do anything for food.

Training them for a milk stand is also good for them, as well as making life easier for you. You can make them mount the stand, then put their head through the front head gap. Then, gently touch their udders. They will get jumpy because they are bound to think you will hurt them. Make sure you tell them you will not hurt them. Repeat this process twice a week. Two weeks before kidding you will need to do it every day. In this way they will become accommodating and will trust you.

Training them to be led or leashed is also good. Some goats, however, will attempt to drag you with them. Don't pull your goats when they are on a leash; move them sideways, and then pull gently. They will walk with you. Sometimes, you will need some extra force to make them walk; in that case, wrap the cord around your body's front, and then walk. You can also move them sideways, turn in a circle and then pull, all the while using your body's strength, and this will make them walk with you. Another method for dealing with the problem of a goat trying to drag you is when they get ahead, you turn around, and now you are leading them. Your goats need this training such as this to be repeated.

When you have electric wire fencing, you will need to train them on it. This will require a companion, someone you can rely upon, so that when things go wrong, this person can quickly turn the system down. Once you start training, your goat will be zapped on their nose, which will give them, in a very direct fashion, the idea to not go near the fence. You can also train the whole pack together because they learn by watching each other. When they do get zapped, they will mostly run backwards from the fence, but babies might not; they might, in their sudden confusion, actually run forwards and possibly become tangled up in the fence. This is where your companion will come in handy. Your goat will understand the electric fencing, but don't force them to it.

The health and wellbeing of your goat is always of key concern. You will need your goats to be healthy because they, in turn, will reward you by giving surplus amounts of good quality milk. Methods to achieve this include brushing, bathing, and clipping. Start with brushing. You will need a curry comb and a soft brush. First use a curry comb, and start gliding it in circular motions from the neck to their legs and abdomen. Then, repeat this process with a soft brush. This helps remove any tangles, knots, insects, and dandruff, and also increases blood flow.

The goat requires bathing next. Wet their whole coat, and lather it, using any liquid shampoo or soap. Make sure it won't get into their eyes. Then rinse it all off. After this comes clipping. Clipping is especially necessary in summer because cropped hair will keep them warm and away from all the dirt and lice. When you start clipping, make sure you don't hurt them. Brushing and bathing should be done every now and then. As for clipping, it depends on the growth of their coat.

Their hooves also need trimming. But it should be done by an expert because there is a blood vessel in their foot, and, if you lack the experience, you can damage that vessel. Trimming is usually done four times a year. When your goat habitually moves on solid ground and hard rocks, those surfaces help to wear their hooves off, but when they mostly roam around in wetlands, lush grass and pasture, then this doesn't happen on its own, and you will need to take care of it for them.

Daily exercises for your goat are a must. It will keep them active, their digestive system will work properly, and they, in turn, will give you excellent results with their milk. Your livestock guardian can go behind them on your command, and this is a kind of exercise. You can also run with them, and do some laps. Running will burn off their fat, and will also help in creating a strong bond between you. You can make them do some funny tricks and jumps as well. Take advantage of whatever space you have. When your goat starts panting, then it is a sign to stop. Don't make them overdo it.

It is also imperative to watch your goats closely for any signs of unhealthiness. They are resilient animals, but still you will be well advised to observe them closely. When your goat won't eat properly, then it is a sign of their stress. Healthy goats have perked up ears, shiny, glossy and sharp eyes, and straight shoulders. If you find any of these elements missing, it's an indication of something wrong.

Goats are very active animals. They like to move around, and peek into things, and when they don't do that, or they isolate themselves from the entire herd, it is a definite sign of something not right. If you see them idling around, and lying down more than necessary, then check up on them. When you find them bleating excessively, screaming, or hear odd cries, then they are not right. The kidding time is also noisy sometimes, but that is a more natural situation.

When you see them trembling and shivering, or find their temperature is either too high or too low, and then they are clearly suffering from something. Bloating is also a sign that they are overfeeding themselves. You might see them walking awkwardly, or limping, or if they are not urinating properly, or their feces are strange, then these are the sure signs of unhealthiness.

The following are some common health problems, and knowing them would give you an edge, and you will be able to control these situations if they ever appear.

Overeating is a disease where the animal gets Clostridium Perfringens infection, and dies. The healthiest animal of your herd would suddenly drop dead. There is a vaccine to prevent it.

When a rusty nail makes a puncture wound on a human's skin, we would naturally take a Tetanus injection. The same is the case with goats. This organism, Clostridium Tetani is very commonly found in dirt, so the only prevention is the vaccine.

Sore mouth is also common among goats and sheep. You will notice a scab right at the corner of your goat's mouth. It is exactly like chicken pox in humans. It heals on its own. But there is also a vaccine against it. Urinary Calculi is also another common disease in which stones are found in the goat's urethra. These stones form because of diet imbalance, some goat treats, and lack of water.

Pregnancy Toxemia is commonly found in fat goats, and in pregnant goats who are 3 months away from their delivery. Because of a lot of rain, their glucose level drops, and they get this. Electrolytes help in this case.

Coccidiosis is a parasite which is present in all the animals, but they will not show any clinical signs. But when they get stressed, this organism suddenly multiplies. Medications are available.

Caseous Lymphadenitis (CL) is caused by Corynebacterium. In this, you see a golf ball-sized lump around their throat, or sometimes in front of their shoulders. Remove it, or flush it with iodine, and they are good.

Contagious foot rot is caused by Fusobacterium necrophorum. This organism is commonly found in wet lands and greenery. Antibiotics and Copper Sulphate are used to treat it. Some parts of the world are deficient in Selenium and that's where this White Muscle disease is common in goats. Supplements are given to counteract this deficiency.

Goats have a specific breeding time which usually starts around fall, and ends in late winter. It's from August to late January. Some goats, mostly meat goats, breed all year, but it is not good for their health because it takes a toll on their body. During breeding time, female goats get receptive and let male goats breed them. However, it is important to know what age is ideal to breed them, and what is the actual process. Male goats are called bucks, whereas female goats are known as does or nannies. Breeders also choose some specific time for breeding because they don't want babies to come all year round. During their breeding time, the female goat goes through a cycle which is called an estrous cycle or heat cycle. A doe gets into heat from 12 to 36 hours every month, which is called the reproductive cycle. The time period between each reproductive cycle is called a heat cycle.

Does are ready to be bred when they are one-year old, or when they get to around 70 to 85 pounds in weight. Weight matters a lot because it determines they are ready to carry babies. A year-old buck can impregnate around 10 does, a 2-year-old around 25, and a 3-year-old around 40 does at a time. When does get in heat, you will see them wagging their tails a lot, they will also bleat ceaselessly, and they will love to hang around bucks. A buck will start urinating on himself, will stink, curl his mouth, and will blabber and sniff unstoppably.

Does stand and let bucks breed them. It is not likely they will conceive the very first time. Sonograms will confirm whether they have conceived or not. After this, the gestation period starts, this is around 140 to 150 days at maximum. It is imperative to take care of their diet during this period. Give them a light diet at the start. Then, after two months, you will increase their diet. Then, during their last 15 days, you will need to increase and incorporate grains into diet for their nutrition. This will help ensure smooth labor. You can consult your vet for further guidance. When your doe gets really big, do watch over them closely, because they usually become uncomfortable and stop eating. Make sure they are at ease in their shelters when the time is near.

When your doe is very close to delivering, you will notice their udders swelling, they will get hard, the babies inside will give the mother's belly a drooping look, their tail ligaments will start to loosen, they will discharge a vaginal fluid, and right before birth, she will separate herself from the entire herd. They will paw the ground, and you will notice contractions. Then they will push the baby out. You will see a bag coming out and a baby will be in it. If you see your goat is having difficulty in pushing, then you can go and help her. Sometimes babies get stuck inside, and the situation gets complicated, so make sure you're ready for it, and have an emergency plan. Sometimes goats die during birthing, and that's why you must be ready to take things under control. After birthing, the mother will lick her babies clean, and warm them to create a motherly bond. If she doesn't, then you put her children in front of her, and remind her. Placenta will be expelled slowly. It will eject in about two days. Eating their own placenta is normal for them. It is actually good for their health. Bounce your doe's belly, and make sure no baby or placenta is in there anymore. A doe likely breeds about 3 babies at a time.

Keep your buck separately once breeding is done, and even before kidding. Make sure you record your goats' kidding time, number of kids, how many died, and the amount of milk they give every day.

Taking care of newborn babies is important, or they will die because of hypothermia. When it is cold, you will need to bring them somewhere warm. You can also use a heater, but make sure the animals don't get too near it. Cut their umbilical cord to 1.5 inches and dip it into Iodine solution to avoid any infection. Babies come around to sucking their mother's udders, but if not, you should help them. Usually, the mother nurses them, if not, then you will need to bottle feed them with milk which has a replacement of their mother's.

Babies need milk feeding four times a day till they are 4 weeks old, then you can gradually decrease it to two, and incorporate solid food in the form of dry hay, grass and grains. Don't overfeed them, or they will have digestive issues. Keep baby goats separately for their safety, but occasionally allow them to mingle with the herd. Keep the fencing secured and tight because predators attack babies very easily. If you have high-extension wiring or fencing, then you will need to be extra careful to train them to keep away from it. Do this as quickly as possible.

There are also a lot of mistakes people do. Very common mistakes which, at the time, they didn't realize until some misfortune hits them. They make mistakes while purchasing a goat, finding a breed, setting up a homestead or a farm, feeding them, securing them, handling them, taking care of them, training them, breeding them. When you purchase a goat, make sure to avoid these errors, and thereby avert any disaster to you or your animal.

Goats are herd animals, and very social, so avoid getting just a single goat. Otherwise, they will be lonely, and will try to escape, In some cases, they do escape and you will lose your animal forever. When you are setting up a farm or homestead, you can't always control natural factors, but do make sure you check out those factors which you can control. Don't ever buy a goat on an impulse. Do your research properly, and don't just go and get yourself a goat without looking properly at everything, and asking everything. Go beyond Craigslist. Search your local breeders. It’s untrue that raising animals naturally stops them getting sick. This is a myth, and believing in it is a mistake. They will get sick, and you will have to get them proper treatment, even by artificial means.

We always search online when we want to get something, but the Internet is not always reliable, unless someone has a lot of expertise in something and has been doing it for a long time. The same is the case with goats. Ask your locals; they will be able to guide you properly. Read books and magazines, and then go to the internet. Whatever is popular on Google isn't always correct. People say when you feed your goats properly, they will not eat poisonous plants. This is not true. They will still eat them. So, when you set up a homestead, if there are some poisonous plants like Rhododendron, Laurel Mountains or Azaleas, remove them or they will eat them and become ill.

Start on a small scale. People may well be enthusiastic initially, but too much enthusiasm isn't always a good thing. An owner can attempt to be too big, too early, and that just drains the fun out of it, and causes frustration. Whenever you decide to purchase a goat, remember to get an animal whose environment is similar to yours. Otherwise, they won't be able to thrive properly.

People see green land with lush grass, and think this is perfect for their goats. In reality, it is quite the opposite. Parasites and worms live there. If you put your goats on wet and grassy lands, they will develop internal worms and foot rot. Dry land and dry patches are good for them.

When there is a worm problem, make sure to figure out deworming. Once you have given the medication, monitor its progress. If it is not working, switch to some other medication. There is no need to waste more time on something that isn't working. Worms develop resistance against medications, so it is good to rotate the prescription. Get yourself a microscope, and do all the fecal tests yourself. This will quicken the whole process.

It will save money, your time, and the life of your animal.

.

New owners make the mistake of not getting a livestock guardian. When your animals wander around, predators will attack, so a guardian will let not let them enter the area. If you want to make a good herd, invest in your buck and doe. They will pass their health and traits to their kids, which, in turn, will give you a great herd. Write everything down. The amount of milk per day, how many babies a doe kidded, and how many died. Otherwise, you will start forgetting once the herd numbers increase.

When you feed your goat dry bales of hay, make sure to cut the net around it, otherwise they will tangle themselves in it and get hurt. Don't overfeed your goat. They love grains, which are the main cause of bloating, and if not treated in time, they might also die. Avoid those goat treats you see in the market; don't indulge them with those. They are not good for their health. Their main food is grass, dry hay, and grains; these are good for them.

Don't breed your does all year round. It is dangerous for their health. Pregnancy takes some energy from them, so it is recommended to do it once a year. Weight is necessary to decide whether a doe is ready to breed or not. Don't breed a buck and doe that are not equal in weight and size because they will hurt each other during the process. Birthing is a difficult process. There is a chance that Does can die during kidding. So, when your doe is due, make sure you tackle the situation if anything goes wrong. Panicking at the last minute won't help your animal; you will need an emergency plan. Newborn babies need immediate care, or they will die of hypothermia or infections.

Having some general medications at hand would save a lot of trouble at the last minute, and you won't have to travel to your vet for every small thing.

Avoiding these mistakes would make this whole experience very interesting and fun.

Chapter Summary

- Don't purchase goats without thorough research about the animal, without asking all the important questions, and getting all the information about the breed you want to get.

- Kikos are great when you want to buy male goats. Nigerian Dwarf goats, Pygmy goats and Boer goats are great dairy and meat goats respectively.

- The ideal adoption age of a baby goat is at least 2 weeks because by that time they would have nursed enough of their mother's milk.

- Don't overfeed your goats whether they are baby goats or adult goats. This will be hard for their digestive system, and is a major cause for bloating.

- Setting up a warm, safe and secure shelter, is a must before getting a goat.

- Don't ever get a single goat because they get lonely and depressed. They will escape, or get stressed, and you will be in for a disaster.

- Goats need special fencing which is a 4-inch square netting. 6-inch square fencing will allow them to put their head through and get hurt.

- While handling your goats and training them, aggressive behavior and any kind of force will not do anything, rather it will stress your animal, and they will not cooperate with you.

- Patience is the main element when you want to keep goats in your homestead or farm.

- Goats are usually very resilient animals, but there are some common diseases which they can catch, so some vaccines and medications should be to hand. This will save you some hassle, and will buy you time.

- Pregnant goats require a quality nutritional program which will help them in their gestation period and during labor.

- Goats are clever animals, but you will need to show them step-by-step what you want them to do.

- When they do well, and cooperate, giving them some goat treats will encourage them more. They love almonds, carrots, vegetable peels, and flatbreads.

- After birth, newborn babies need immediate care, because they get dehydrated and can die of hypothermia.

- Don't breed your does throughout the year, as this is dangerous for their health.

- When you want to breed your doe, they must be 1-year-old, and their weight should be around 70 to 85 pounds. This is necessary, otherwise your doe will die during pregnancy.

- When you have high-tensile wire as your fencing, you will need to train them on it, so they will know to not get near it.

- Taking care of your goat is very important as it will determine the quality and amount of milk they will produce.

- Invest in good quality animals for your doe and your buck. They will pass these traits on to their babies, and your herd will get fit and healthy.

- Internal worming is a common problem in goats, so when you notice this in their feces, start deworming immediately.

- Goats are very active animals, so when you see them limping, bleating in odd ways, lying around, and not eating properly, these are the signs of their unhealthiness.

FINAL WORDS

My idea behind writing this book is to come up with something which is not discussed much. I have seen quite a number of works on many animals, but while researching, I didn't see much on goats. It made me wonder why so few people know about these animals. It inspired me to come up with something which would benefit people on a large scale. Goats are cute, funny, curious, and intelligent creatures, and I wanted my readers to know about this as much as I do.

I decided to write a book myself. Of course, doing all the research was not something I did overnight. It took me days and countless nights. The exertion was real, but I wanted to be thorough, so that my readers wouldn't be misled. I wanted to compile each and every aspect of goats in detail, so this book would not only be useful for the students out there, but also for those who want to have goats, and who might find it extremely hard to get all the information they need in one place.

I have discussed everything from their history, how they came into being, to purchasing the right kind of breed, what to see while buying, to shelter, to handling, to caring, feeding, training, breeding, tips, tricks, mistakes and all the other major and minor matters. The idea of their history is a creation of my own mind, how I think goats came into this world, and I am expecting that it will also pique my readers' interest. I am hoping and anticipating that this work of mine will be of use for all my readers out there.

Also, while researching and writing this book, I myself have learned so much. I've discovered things I didn't know existed, and so many other tiny details. After completing this work, I was very happy to finally see my idea in my hands, and ready to spread some knowledge of these amazing animals. If you find this book to be of any use to you, then please do share it with others, so that they can also gain something from this.

www.ingramcontent.com/pod-product-compliance
Lightning Source LLC
Chambersburg PA
CBHW052356060726
47592CB00020B/2448

* 9 7 8 1 9 5 1 3 4 5 2 0 4 *